Sir Lewis Morri

Songs of Two Worlds

Sir Lewis Morri

Songs of Two Worlds

ISBN/EAN: 9783744777315

Printed in Europe, USA, Canada, Australia, Japan

Cover: Foto ©Thomas Meinert / pixelio.de

More available books at **www.hansebooks.com**

SONGS OF TWO WORLDS.

BY

A NEW WRITER.

Φωνᾶντα συνετοῖσιν.

LONDON:

HENRY S. KING & CO., 65, CORNHILL.

1871.

SONGS OF TWO WORLDS.

SOUL-MUSIC.

My soul is as a bird
Singing in fair weather,
Deep in shady woodlands through the
evening's dewy calm ;
Every glossy feather
On her full throat stirred,
As she pours out, rapt, unconscious, all
the sweetness of her psalm ;
Mounting high, and higher, higher,
Soaring now, now falling, dying;
Now through silvery pauses sighing ;
Throbbing now with joyous strife,
And rushing tides of love and life,
Till some ray of heavenly fire
Shot obliquely through the shade,
Pierces her ; and lo ! the strain

Of the music she has made
Fills her with a sudden pain.

Then she forgets to sing
Her former songs of gladness;
Sitting mute in silence sweeter than the
    old forgotten lays;
Till anon some note of sadness,
Long-drawn, languishing,
Faint at first, swells onward slowly to a
    subtler depth of praise,
As the low, wild, minor, broken
By the ghosts of gayer fancies,
Like a rippling stream advances,
Till the full tide grown too deep,
Whispers first, then falls asleep.
Then, as souls with no word spoken
Grow together, she, mute and still,
Thrills through with a secret voice,
Which the farthest heaven can fill,
And constrains her to rejoice.

And the passer-by who hears,
Not the burst of pleasure,

Swelling upward, sweet, spontaneous, to
    the portals of the sky,
    But a chastened measure,
    Low and full of tears ;
And anon the voiceless silence, when the
    last notes sink and die,
    Deems some influence malign,
    Checks the current of the song ;
    For that none are happy long.
    Nay; but to the rapt soul come
    Sounds that strike the singer dumb,
    And the silence is Divine ;
    For when heaven gives back the strain,
    All it's joyous tones are o'er ;
    First the low sweet notes of pain,
    Then, the singer sings no more.

———o———

LOVE'S MIRROR.

I SEE myself reflected in thine eyes,
The dainty mirrors set in golden frame
Of eyelash, quiver with a sweet surprise,
    And most ingenuous shame.

Like Eve, who hid her from the dread command,
Deep in the dewy blooms of paradise ;
So thy shy soul, love calling, fears to stand
    Discovered at thine eyes.

Or, like a tender little fawn, which lies
Asleep amid the fern, and waking, hears
Some careless footstep drawing near, and flies,
    Yet knows not what she fears.

So shrinks thy soul; but, dearest, shrink not so ;
Look thou into mine eyes as I in thine :
So our reflected souls shall meet and grow,
    And each with each combine

In something nobler ; as when one has laid
Opposite mirrors on a cottage wall;
And lo ! the never-ending colonnade,
    The vast palatial hall.

So our twin souls, by one sweet suicide,
  Shall fade into an essence more sublime ;
Living through death, and dying glorified,
  Beyond the touch of time.

———o———   `

ON A YOUNG POET.

HERE lay him down in peace to take his rest,
Who tired of singing ere the day was done,
A little time, a little, beneath the sun,
He tarried and gave forth his artless song.
The bird that sings with the dawn, sings not for long,
Only when dew is on the grass his breast
Quivers, but his voice is silent long ere noon.
So sang he once, but might not long sustain
The high pure note of youth, for soon, too soon !
He ceased to know the sweet creative pain
Made still one voice, amid the clamorous strife,
And proved no more the joys or pains of life.

And better so than that his voice should fail,
And sink to earth, and lose its heavenlier tone ;
Perchance, if he had stayed, the sad world's moan,
The long low discord of incessant wrong,

Had marred the perfect cadence of his song,
And made a grosser music to prevail.
But now it falls as pure upon the ear,
As sings the brown bird to the star of eve,
Or child's voice in grey minster quiring clear.
Rather then, give we thanks for him than grieve,
Thoughts of pure joys which but in memory live,
More joy than lower present joys can give.

For him, deep rest or high spontaneous strains ;
For us, fierce strife and low laborious song ;
For him, truth's face shining out clear and strong ;
For us half lights, thick clouds, and darkling days.
No longer walks his soul in mortal ways,
Nor thinks our thoughts, nor feels our joys or pains;
Nor doubts our doubts, nor any more pursues.
Knowing all things, the far-off searchless cause,
Nor thrills with art, or nature's fairest hues,
Gazing on absolute beauty's inmost laws ;
Or lies for ever sunk in dreamless sleep,
Nor recks of us ;—and therefore 'tis we weep.

But surely if he sleep, some fair faint dream,
Some still small whisper from his ancient home ;

On a Young Poet.

Not joy, nor pain, but mixt of each shall come,
Or if he wake, the thought of earthly days
Shall add a tender sweetness to his praise ;
Tempering the unbroken joyance of his theme.
And by-and-by the time shall come when we,
Laden with all our lives, once more shall meet,
Like friends, who after infinite wastes of sea,
Look in each other's eyes ; and lo! the sweet
Sad fount of memory to its depths is stirred,
And the past lives again, without a word.

Mourn not for him! perchance he lends his voice
To swell the fulness of the eternal psalm ;
Or haply, wrapt in nature's holy calm,
Safe hid within the fruitful womb of earth,
He ripens slowly to a higher birth.
Mourn not for him! but let your souls rejoice.
We know not what we shall be, but are sure
The spark once kindled by the eternal breath,
Goes not out quite, but somewhere doth endure
In that strange life we blindly christen death.
Somewhere he is, though where we cannot tell ;
But wheresoe'er God hides him, it is well.

TO THE SETTING SUN.

STAY, O sweet day, nor fleet so fast away ;
　For now it is that life revives again,
As the red tyrant sinks beneath the hill ;
　And now soft dews refresh the arid plain ;
And now the fair bird's voice begins to thrill ;
　With hidden dolours making sweet her strain,
And wakes the woods that all day were so still.

Stay, O sweet day, nor fleet so fast away ;
　For now the rose and all fair flowers that blow,
Give out sweet odours to the perfumed air,
　And the white palace marbles blush and glow,
And the low, ivy-hidden cot shows fair.
　Why are time's feet so swift, and ours so slow ?
Haste, laggard ! night will fall ere you are there.

Stay, O sweet day, nor fleet so fast away ;
　Soon the pale full-faced moon will slowly climb
Up the steep sky and quench the star of love.
　Moonlight is fair, but fairer far the time

When through the leaves the golden shafts above
　　Slope, and the minster sounds its faint low chime,
And the long shadows lengthen through the grove.

Stay, O sweet day, nor fleet so fast away ;
　　For, hark ! the chime throbs from the darkling tower ;
Soon for the last time shall my love be here :
　　Fair day, renew thy rays for one brief hour.
O sweet day, tarry for us, tarry near ;
　　To-morrow, love and time will lose their power,
And sighs be mine, and the unbidden tear.

Stay, O sweet day, nor fleet so fast away.
　　But, ah ! thou may'st not ; in the far-off west
Impatient lovers weary till you rise :
　　Or may be caring nought thou traversest
The plains betwixt thee and thy final skies :
　　Go, then ; though darkness come, we shall be blest,
Keeping sweet daylight, in each other's eyes.

———o———

•

THE TREASURE OF HOPE.

O FAIR bird, singing in the woods,
    To the rising and the setting sun,
Does ever any throb of pain
    Thrill through thee ere thy song be done :
Because the summer fleets so fast ;
    Because the autumn fades so soon ;
Because the deadly winter treads
    So closely on the steps of June ?

O sweet maid, opening like a rose
    In love's mysterious, honeyed air,
Dost think sometimes the day will come
    When thou shalt be no longer fair :
When love will leave thee and pass on
    To younger and to brighter eyes ;
And thou shalt live unloved, alone,
    A dull life, only dowered with sighs ?

O brave youth, panting for the fight,
    To conquer wrong and win thee fame,

Dost see thyself grown old and spent,
  And thine a still unhonoured name :
When all thy hopes have come to naught,
  And all thy fair schemes droop and pine ;
And wrong still lifts her hydra heads
  To fall to stronger arms than thine ?

Nay ; song and love and lofty aims
  May never be where faith is not ;
Strong souls within the present live ;
  The future veiled,—the past forgot :
Grasping what is, with hands of steel,
  They bend what shall be, to their will ;
And blind alike to doubt and dread,
  The End, for which they are, fulfil.

———o———

THE LEGEND OF FAITH.

THEY say the Lord of time and all the worlds,
Came to us once, a feeble, new-born child;
All-wise, yet dumb; weak, though omnipotent ·
Surely a heaven-sent vision, for it tells
How innocence is godlike.   And the Lord
Renews, through childhood, to our world-dimmed eyes,
The half forgotten splendours of the skies.

And because motherhood is sacreder
And purer far than any fatherhood,
White flowers are fairer than red fruit, and sense
Brings some retributive pain; the virgin queen
Sits 'mid the stars, and cloistered courts are filled
With vain regrets, dead lives, and secret sighs,
And the long pain of weary litanies.

And because we, who stand upon the shore,
See the cold wave sweep up and take with it
White spotless souls, and others lightly soiled,
Yet with no stain God deems indelible:
These are His saints mighty to intercede,

Those in some dim far country tarry, and there
Are purified ; and both are reached by prayer.

And as the faith once given changes not,
But we are weak as water ; yet is life
A process, and where growth is not is death.
God gave His priests infallible power to tell
The true faith as it is, and how it grew :
And lo ! the monstrous cycle shows complete,
And the Church brings the nations to her feet.

———o———

BY THE SEA.

A LITTLE country churchyard,
　　On the verge of a cliff by the sea ;
Ah ! the thoughts of the long years past and gone
　　That the vision brings back to me.

For two ways led from the village,—
　　One, by the rippled sands,
With their pink shells fresh from the ebbing wave
　　For childish little hands.

And one 'mid the heath, and the threat'ning
    Loud bees with the yellow thighs,
And, twinkling out of the golden furze,
    The marvellous butterflies.

And the boom of the waves on the shingle,
    And the hymn of the lark to the sun ;
Made Sabbath sounds of their own, ere the chime
    Of the church-going bell had begun.

I remember the churchyard studded
    With peasants who loitered and read
The sad little legends, half effaced,
    On the moss-grown tombs of the dead.

And the gay graves of little children,
    Fashioned like tiny cots ;
With their rosemary and southernwood,
    And blue-eyed forget-me-nots.

Till the bell by degrees grew impatient,
    Then ceased as the parsonage door
Opened wide for the surpliced vicar,
    And we loitered and talked no more.

I remember the cool, dim chancel,
    And the drowsy hum of the prayers ;
And the rude psalms vollied from sea-faring throats,
    As if to take heaven unawares.

Till, when sermon-time came, by permission
    We stole out among the graves,
And saw the great ocean a-blaze in the sun,
    And heard the deep roar of the waves.

And clung very close together,
    As we spelt out with wonder and tears,
How a boy lay beneath who was drowned long ago,
    And was " Aged eleven years."

And heard, with a new-born terror,
    The first surge of the infinite Sea,
Whose hither-shore is the shore of Death,
    And whose further, the Life to be.

Did the sea swallow up little children ?
    Could God see the wickedness done ?
Nor spare one swift-winged seraph to save
    From the thousands around His throne ?

Was he still scarce older than we were,
  Still only a boy of eleven?
Were child-angels children always
  In the beautiful courts of heaven?

Ah me! of those childish dreamers,
  One has solved the dark riddle since then:
And knows the dread secret which none may know
  Who walk in the ways of men.

The other has seen the splendour
  And mystery fading away;
Too wise or too dull to take thought or care
  For aught but the needs of the day.

———o———

VOICES.

Oh! sometimes when the solemn organ rolls
Its stream of sound down gray historic aisles;
Or the full, high-pitched struggling symphony
Pursues the fleeting melody in vain:
Like a fawn through shadowy groves, or heroine
Voiced like a lark, pours out in burning song

Her love or grief; or when, to the rising stars
Linked village maidens chant the hymn of eve;
Or Sabbath concourse, flushed and dewy-eyed
Booms its full bass; or before tasks begun,
Fresh childish voices sanctify the morn :
My eyes grow full, my heart forgets to beat.
What is this mystic yearning fills my being ?

Hark! the low music wakes, and soft and slow
Wanders at will through flowery fields of sound;
Climbs gentle hills, and sinks in sunny vales,
And stoops to cull sweet way-side blooms, and weaves
A dainty garland; then, grown tired, casts down
With careless hand the fragrant coronal,
And child-like sings itself to sleep.

                             Anon
The loud strain rises like a strong knight armed,
Battling with wrong; or passionate seer of God
Scathing with tongue of fire the hollow shows,
The vain deceits of men ; or law-giver,
Parting in thunder from the burning hill
With face aflame; or with fierce rush of wings

And blazing brand, upon the crest of Sin,
The swift archangel swooping ; or the roll
Which follows on the lightning ;—all are there
In that great hurry of sound.
                              And then the voice
Grows thinner like a lark's, and soars and soars,
And mounts in circles, higher, higher, higher,
Up to heaven's gate, and lo ! the unearthly song
Thrills some fine inner chord, and the swift soul,
Eager and fluttering like a prisoned bird,
Breaks from its cage, and soars aloft to join
The enfranchised sound, and for a moment seems
To touch on some dim border-land of being,
Full of high thought and glorious enterprise
And vague creative fancies, till at length
Waxed grosser than the thin ethereal air,
It sinks to earth again.
                         And then a strain
Sober as is the tender voice of home,
Unbroken like a gracious life, and lo
Young children sit around me, and the love
I never knew is mine, and so my eyes
Grow full, and all my being is thrilled with tears.

What is this strange new life, this finer sense,
This passionate exaltation, which doth force
Like the weird Indian juggler, instantly
My soul from seed to flower, from flower to fruit,
Which lifts me out of self, and bids me tread
Without a word, on reeling dizzy heights,
Impossible else, and rise to glorious thoughts,
High hopes, and inarticulate fantasies
Denied to soberer hours. No spoken thought
Of bard or seer can mount so far, or lift
The soul to such transcendent heights, or work
So strong a spell of love, or roll along
Such passionate troubled depths. No painter's hand
Can limn so clear, the luminous air serene
Of Paradise, the halcyon deep, the calm
Of the eternal snows, the eddy and whirl
Of mortal fight, the furious flood let loose
From interlacing hills, the storm which glooms
Over the shoreless sea. Our speech too oft :
Is bound and fettered by such narrow laws,
That words which to one nation pierce the heart,
To another are but senseless sounds, or weak
And powerless to stir the soul ; but this

Speaks with a common tongue, uses a speech
Which all may understand, or if it bear
Some seeds of difference in it, only such
As separates gracious sisters, like in form,
But one by gayer fancies touched, and one
Rapt by sweet graver thoughts alone, and both
Mighty to reach the changing moods of the soul,
Or grave or gay, and though sometimes they be
Mated with unintelligible words,
Or feeble and unworthy, yet can lend
A charm to gild the worthless utterance,
And wing the sordid chrysalis to float
Amid the shining stars.

                              Oh strange sweet power,
Ineffable, oh gracious influence,
I know not whence thou art, but this I know,
Thou holdest in thy hand the silver key .
That can unlock the sacred fount of tears,
Which falling make life green ; the hidden spring
Of purer fancies and high sympathies :
No mirth is thine, thou art too high for mirth,—
Like Him who wept but smiled not : mirth is born
On the low plains of thought best reached by words.

But those who scale the untrodden mountain peak,
Or sway upon the trembling spire, are far
From laughter; so thy gracious power divine,
Not sad but solemn, moves the well of tears,
But not mirth's shallow spring : tears are divine,
But mirth is of the earth, a creature born
Of careless youth and joyance; satisfied
With that which is ; urged by no nobler thirst
For that which might be; pained by no regret
For that which was, but is not : but for thee,
Oh, fair mysterious power, the whole great scheme
Lies open like a book ; and if the charm
Of its high beauty makes thee sometimes gay,
Yet 'tis an awful joy, so mixed with thought,
That even Mirth grows grave, and evermore
The myriad possibilities unfulfilled,
The problem of Creation, the immense
Impenetrable depths of thought, the vague
Perplexities of being, rise to thy lips
And keep thee solemn always.
                              Oh, fair voice,
Oh virginal, sweet interpreter, reveal
Our inner selves to us, lay bare the springs

The hidden depths of being, the high desires
Which lie there unsuspected, the remorse
Which never woke before; unclothe the soul
Of this its shroud of sense, and let it mount,
On the harmonious beat of thy light wings,
Up to those heights where life is so attuned,
So pure and self-concordant; filled so deep
With such pervading beauty that no voice
Breaks the ineffable harmony of being,
And o'er white plain and breathless summit reigns
A silence sweeter than the sweetest sound.

———o———

WEAKNESS MADE STRONG.

IF I were poor and weak,
    Bankrupt of hope, and desolate of love ;
Without a tongue to speak
      The strange dumb thoughts of thee which through
        me move ;
Then would I freely venture, sweet,
To cast my soul down at thy feet.

Or were I proud and great ;
Were all men envious, and all women kind ;
And yet my high estate
Showed poor beside the riches of my mind :
Then would I boldly stoop, to rise
Up to the height of thy dear eyes.

But being not weak nor strong,
Cast in the common mould of coarser clay ;
Sure 't were to do thee wrong
To set my humble homage in thy way,
And cloud thy sunny morn, which I would fain
Keep clear and fair, with my poor private pain.

Only since love and I are so ingrown,
That for my weakness is my love so strong ;
And scarce I know what love's is, what mine own,
Nor whether love or I inspire my song :
Take thou my strength unto thyself, and give
Strength to my weakness, sweet, and bid me live.

—— o ——

WAKING.

OPEN, my soul, thy stately portals wide ;
  Open full wide, and let thy King come in !
How shall he come? In royal pomp and pride,
  Ushered by braying trumpets' clamorous din ;
Clothed round with purple ; crowned with burning gold :
A kingly presence, glorious to behold ?

Nay ; for he is no mortal king, to come
  With trumpet peals and crowds and garish state ;
But silent to the soul he makes his home :
  He enters by some lowly postern gate !
And she, within her chambers far withdrawn,
Cries like the wakeful bird that greets the dawn.

It may be she is seated 'mid the throng,
  Crowned with the flowers of life and youth and health ;
Thrilled through by breathing art or passionate song,
  Or faint with hot pursuit of fame or wealth ;
Rapt by the glorious thoughts of saints or seers,
Or radiant with the blessèd dew of tears.

And then the wicket swings without a sound,
    And lo! a ghostly presence, pale and gray,—
Sad eyes which dwell not on the things around,
    But gaze for ever on the Far-off Day!
Then a low voice, whispering, "Thy King is come;
Rejoice, be glad, for here he makes his home."

Then rises she and hastens to the gate,—
    The royal gate, and there she casts her down :
Prone at his feet bewails her low estate,
    Yet prays him he will enter to his own !
Spurns from her all her robes of pride, and stands,
Knowing her shame, to do her Lord's commands,

Whom with a touch he fashions for her part ;
    Dowers with the precious gifts of bard or sage ;
The hand to fix the dreams of deathless art,
    The imperial will, the patriot's noble rage :
Or fills with such fine affluence of love,
That she grows holy as the saints above.

Then open, O my soul! thy portals wide,
    Open, and let thy Lord and Ruler come ;

Open, if haply he may here abide,
  And make within thee his eternal home.
Open thy gates, thy halls, thine inmost shrine,
Till all are flooded with the Light divine.

——o——

A STORY OF ARGOS.

Two youths of Argos, brave and dutiful :
I tell the simple story of their end.

For when the unfailing cycle of the year
Brought round the appointed season, came report
To where they dwelt among the Argive fields,
They and their mother, pious, full of years,
Revering always all the blessèd Gods,
How Herè's solemn festival was come,
And all who honoured her must needs go up
To do the goddess service. Hearing this,
And knowing that she had short time to live,
Stirred through the aged woman strong desire
If only she might look on Herè's face,
And kneel once more before her, ere the end.

Then, for her limbs were feeble, question rose,
How she might have her wish ?   Their cottage home
Lay many weary leagues of hill and plain
From Argos ;—all the oxen were a-field
At harvest.   So that she might have her wish,
And filled with pious love for her, her sons
Made answer, they would bear her to the shrine,
So she might look on Herè's face again,
And kneel once more before her, ere the end.

So her two sons, such love they bore to her,
Fashioned a shapely litter with their hands,
And laid her with a tender care in it ;
And then they twain, such love they bore to her,
Bent their strong backs and bare her on the road
To Argos ; all the people, as they went,
Admiring.   So they sped across the plain,
Amid the hoary olives, by village street
And way-side temple ; through the tangled vines
And darkling groves, deep pastures filled with kine,
And difficult rocks ; till suddenly they saw,
High upward, on a far-off purple hill,
The shrine of Herè, glimmer like a star.

So they fared on, such love they bore to her,
Till evermore more weary grew the way,
And all the glaring landscape reeled and swam,
And on the olives played a quivering haze,
And like a nightmare showed the far-off shrine,
Distant, unreal, ghostly ; and evermore,
Such darts the great Far-worker aimed at them,
Their eyes grew dim, their hearts throbbed hard and high,
Their youthful limbs hung heavy with the toil ;
Yet with no word of murmur or complaint,
Revering the high service which they owed
To Heré, and their mother, they toiled on,
Each cheering each,—each heartening each with words,
All day until the evening ; till at length
They reached the distant city, wherein they saw
High, on a scarpéd rock, the shining house
Of Heré set above them.   So at last,
Panting as when they ran and won the crown
At Elis ; ere the oxen left the plough
They toiled along the sounding colonnades.
And all the crowd retreating as they came,
Sank on the icy marble of the floor,
Before the large-eyed Heré :—there they lay
Supine, and all their limbs were loosed in sleep.

Then she, their mother, bending reverent knee
To sovereign Heré, full of pious pride,
For that her sons were such ; and knowing well
How hard it is to live a life unstained ;
Prayed, if perchance, the goddess might be pleased
To give them what best gift was hers to give,
And choicest. As she spake, there seemed to come
A softer glance in Heré's awful eyes,—
The prayer was heard. But not on earth they woke.
Two thousand years have past and more, yet still
Men tell the simple story of their end.

———o———

AT HAVRE DE GRACE.

ABOVE the busy Norman town,
   The high precipitous sea-cliffs rise,
And from their summit looking down
   The twin-lights shine with lustrous eyes;
Far out upon the fields of foam,
The first to greet the wanderer home.

Man here has known at last to tame
    Nature's wild forces to his will ;
Those are the lightning's fires which flame,
    From yon high towers with ray so still :
And knowledge, piercing through the night
Of time, has summoned forth the light.

And there, hard by the light-house door,
    The earthly set by the divine ;
At a stone's cast, or scarcely more,
    Rises a little pagan shrine,'
Where the rough seamen come to pray,
And wives, for dear ones far away.

There, on a starry orb, there stands
    A heavenly goddess, proud and fair ;
No infant holds she in her hands
    Which must a queenly sceptre bear.
Nay; wonder not, for this is she
Who rules the fury of the sea.

Star of the sea, they call her, yet
    Liker to Heré doth she show,

Than Aphrodité, rising wet
　From the white waves, with limbs aglow.
Calmer she seems, more pure and sweet,
To the poor kneelers at her feet.

Before her still the vestal fires
　Burn unextinguished day and night ;
And the sweet frankincense expires
　And fair flowers blow, and gems are bright:
For a great power in heaven is she,
This star and goddess of the sea.

Around the temple, everywhere,
　Rude tablets hung, attest her might;
Here the fierce surge she smooths, and there
　Darts downward on a bar of light :
To quench the blazing ship, or save
The shipwrecked from the hungry wave.

And sea-gifts round the shrine are laid,
　Poor offerings, costlier far than gold :
Such as the earlier heathen made,
　To the twin Deities of old,—

Toy ships, shells, coral, glittering spar,
Brought here by grateful hands from far.

A very present help indeed,
    This goddess is to whom they bow ;
We seek Thy face with hearts that bleed,
    And straining eyes, dread Lord ; but Thou
Hidest Thyself so far away,
Our thoughts scarce reach Thee as we pray.

But is this she, whom the still voice
    Of angels greeted in the night;
Bidding the poor maid's heart rejoice,
    With visions hid from wiser sight:
This heathen nymph, this tinselled queen,
First of all mothers who have been ?

Gross hearts and purblind eyes, to make
    An idol of a soul so sweet !
Could you no meaner essence take,
    No brazen image with clay feet ;
No saint from out the crowd of lies,
False signs and shameful prodigies ?

For this one bears too great a name,
    Above all other women blest;
The blessèd mother,—all her fame
    Is His who nestled to her breast:
They do but dull her glory down,
These childless arms, this earthly crown.

Poor peasant mother! scarce a word
    Thou spak'st, the long-drawn years retain;
Only thy full womb bare the Lord;
    Only thou knew'st the joy, the pain:
The high hope seeming quenched in blood
That marked thy awful motherhood.

No trace of all thy life remains,
    From His first childhood to the cross;
A life of little joys and pains,
    Of humble gain and trivial loss:
Contented if the ewes should bear
Twin lambs, or wheat were full in ear.

Or if sometimes the memory
    Of that dread message of the night

Troubled thy soul, there came to thee
New precious duties; till the flight,
The desert sands, the kneeling kings,
Showed but as half-forgotten things.

Or sometimes, perhaps, while pondering all
In thy fond heart of word and deed,
Some shade of doubt on thee would fall,
Still faithful to the older creed :
Could this thy Son indeed be He,
This child who prattled at thy knee?

And of thy after-life, thy age,
Thy death, no record; not a line
On all the fair historic page
To mark the life these hold divine :
Only some vague tradition, faint
As the sick story of a saint.

But thou no longer art to-day
The sweet maid-mother, fair and pure;
Vast time-worn reverend temples gray,
Throne thee in majesty obscure;

And long aisles stretch in minsters high,
'Twixt thee, fair peasant, and the sky.

They seek to honour thee, who art
    Beyond all else a mother indeed;
With hateful vows that blight the heart,
    With childless lives, and souls that bleed :
As if their dull hymns' barren strain
Could fill a mother with aught but pain !

To the gross earth they bind thee down
    With coils of fable, chain on chain ;
From plague or war to save the town ;
    To give, or hold ; the sun, or rain ;
To whirl through air a favourite shrine,—
These are thy functions, and divine.

And see, in long procession rise
    The fair Madonnas of all time ;
They gaze from sweet maternal eyes,
    The dreams of every Christian clime :
Brown girls and icy queens, the breast
And childish lips proclaim them blest.

Till as the gradual legend grew,
    Born without stain, and scorning death ;
Heavenward thou soarest through the blue,
    While saints and seers aspire beneath :
And fancy-nurtured cam'st to be
Queen over sky and earth and sea.

Oh, sin ! oh, shame ! oh, folly ! Rise;
    Poor heathen, think to what you bow ;
Consider, beyond God's equal skies,
    What pains that faithful soul must know,—
She a poor peasant on the throne
Raised for the Lord of Life, alone.

O sweet ! O heart of hearts ! O pure
    Above all purest maids of earth !
O simple child, who didst endure
    The burden of that awful birth :
Heart, that the keenest sword didst know,
Soul bowed by alien loads of woe !

Sweet soul! have pity; intercede,
    Oh mother of mothers, pure and meek;

They know no evil,—rise and plead
    For these poor wandering souls and weak ;
Tear off those pagan rags, and lead
Their worship where 'tis due indeed.

For wheresoever there is home,
    And mothers yearn with sacred love,
There, since from Heaven itself they come,
    Are symbols of the life above :
Again the sweet maid-mother mild,
Again the God-begotten child.

———o———

WHEN I AM DEAD.

WHEN I am dead and turned to dust,
Let men say what they will, I care not aught ;
Let them say I was careless, indolent,
Wasted the precious hours in dreaming thought,
Did not the good I might have done, but spent
My soul upon myself,—sometimes let rise
Thick mists of earth betwixt me and the skies :
What must be must.

But not that I betrayed a trust ;
Broke some girl's heart, and left her to her shame ;
Sneered young souls out of faith ; rose by deceit ;
Lifted by credulous mobs to wealth and fame ;
Waxed fat while good men waned, by lie and cheat;
Cringed to the strong; oppressed the poor and weak :
When men say this, may some find voice to speak,
Though I am dust.

———o———

LOVE'S SUICIDE.

ALAS for me for that my love is dead !
    Sunk fathom-deep, and may not rise again ;
Self-murdered, vanished, fled beyond recall,
    And this is all my pain.

'Tis not that she I loved is gone from me,
    She lives and grows more lovely day by day;
Not Death could kill my love, but though she lives,
    My love has died away.

Nor was it that a form or face more fair
  Forswore my troth, for so my love had proved
Eye-deep alone, not rooted in the soul ;
  And 'twas not thus I loved.

Nor that by too long dalliance with delight
  And recompense of love, my love had grown
Surfeit with sweets, like some tired bee that flags
  'Mid roses over-blown.

None of these slew my love, but some cold wind,
  Some chill of doubt, some shadowy dissidence
Born out of too great concord, did o'ercloud
  Love's subtle inner sense.

So one sweet changeless chord, too long sustained,
  Falls at its close into a lower tone :
So the swift train, sped on the long, straight way,
  Sways, and is overthrown.

For difference is the soul of life and love,
  And not the barren oneness weak souls prize :
Rest springs from strife, and dissonant chords beget
  Divinest harmonies.

———o———

THE RIVER OF LIFE.

BRIGHT with unnumbered laughters, and swollen by a
    thousand tears,

Rushes along, through upland and lowland, the river of
    life ;

Sometimes foaming and broken, and sometimes silent
    and slumbrous,

Sometimes through rocky glens, and sometimes through
    flowery plains.

Sometimes the mountains draw near, and the black depths
    swirl at their bases,

Sometimes the limitless meads fade on the verge of the
    sky,

Sometimes the forests stand round, and the great trees
    cast terrible shadows,

Sometimes the golden wheat waves, and girls fill their
    pitchers and sing.

Always the same strange flow, through changes and
    chances unchanging,

Always—in youth and in age, in calm and in tempest
    the same—

Whether it sparkle transparent and give back the blue
  like a mirror,
Or sweep on turbid with flood, and black with the
  garbage of towns—
Whether the silvery scale of the minnow flash on the
  pebbles,
Or whether the poisonous ooze cling for a shroud round
  the dead—
Whether it struggle through shoals of white blooms and
  feathery grasses,
Or bear on its bosom the hulls of ocean-tost navies—the
  same.

Flow on, O mystical river, flow on through desert and
  city ;
Broken or smooth, flow onward into the Infinite sea.
Who knows what urges thee on, what dark laws and
  cosmical forces
Stain thee or keep thee pure, and bring thee at last to thy
  goal ?
What is the cause of thy rest or unrest, of thy foulness
  or pureness ?
What is the secret of life, or the painful riddle of death ?

Why is it better to be than to cease, to flow on than to
stagnate?

Why is the river-stream sweet, while the sea is as bitter
as gall?

Surely we know not at all, but the cycle of Being is
eternal,

Life is eternal as death, tears are eternal as joy.

As the stream flowed, it will flow; though 'tis sweet, yet
the sea will be bitter:

Foul it with filth, yet the deltas grow green and the ocean
is clear.

Always the sun and the winds will strike its broad surface
and gather

Some purer drops from its depths, to float in the clouds
of the sky;—

Soon these shall fall once again, and replenish the full-
flowing river.

Roll round then, O mystical cycle! flow onward, ineffable
stream!

—o—

A HEATHEN HYMN.

O LORD, the Giver of my days,
My heart is ready, my heart is ready;
I dare not hold my peace, nor pause,
For I am fain to sing Thy praise.

I praise Thee not, with impious pride,
For that Thy partial hand has given
Bounties of wealth or form or brain,
Good gifts to other men denied.

Nor weary Thee with blind request,
For fancied goods Thy hand withholds;
I know not what to wish or fear,
Nor aught but that Thy will is best.

Not whence I come, nor whither I go,
Nor wherefore I am here, I know;
Nor if my life's tale ends on earth,
Or mounts to bliss, or sinks to woe.

Nor know I aught of Thee, O Lord ;
Behind the veil Thy face is hidden :
We faint, and yet Thy face is hidden ;
We cry,—Thou answerest not a word.

But this I know, O Lord, Thou art,
And by Thee I too live and am ;
We stand together, face to face,
Thou the great whole, and I the part.

We stand together, soul to soul,
Alone amidst Thy waste of worlds ;
Unchanged, though all creation fade,
And Thy swift suns forget to roll.

Wherefore, because my life is Thine,
Because, without Thee I were not ;
Because, as doth the sea, the sun,
My nature gives back the Divine.

Because my being with ceaseless flow
Sets to Thee as the brook to the sea ;
Turns to Thee, as the flower to the sun,
And seeks what it may never know.

Because, without me Thou hadst been
For ever, seated midst Thy suns ;
Marking the soulless cycles turn,
Yet wert Thyself unknown, unseen.

I praise Thee, everlasting Lord,
In life and death, in heaven and hell :
What care I, since indeed Thou art,
And I the creature of Thy word.

Only if such a thing may be :
When all Thy infinite will is done,
Take back the soul Thy breath has given.
And let me lose myself in Thee.

— o —

IN TRAFALGAR SQUARE.

UNDER the picture gallery wall,
As a sea-leaf clings to a wave-worn rock,
Nor shrinks from the surging impetuous shock
Of the breakers which gather and whiten and fall,—
A child's form crouches, nor seems to heed
.The ceaseless eddy and whirl of men :
Men and women with hearts that bleed,
Men and women of wealth and fame,
High in honour, or sunk in shame,
Pass on like phantoms, and pass again,
And he lies there like a weed.

A child's form, said I ; but looking again
It is only the form that is childish now,
For age has furrowed the low dull brow,
And marked the pale face with its lines of pain.
Yet but few years have fled, since I first passed by,
For a dwarf's life is short if you go by the sun,
And marked in worn features and lustreless eye
Some trace of youth's radiance, though faint and thin ;

But now, oh, strange jest! there's a beard to his chin.
And he lies there, grown old ere his youth is done,
With his poor limbs bent awry.

What a passer-by sees, is a monstrous head,
With a look in the eyes as of those who gaze
On some far-off sight with a dumb amaze ;
A face as pale as the sheeted dead,
A frail body propped on a padded crutch,
And lean long fingers, which flutter the keys
Of an old accordion, returning their touch
With some poor faint echoes of popular song,
Trivial at all times and obsolete long,
Psalm-tunes, and African melodies,
Not differing very much.

And there he sits nightly in heat and cold,
When the fountains fall soft on the stillness of June,
Or when the sharp East sings its own shrill tune,
Patiently playing and growing old.
The long year waxes and wanes, the great
Flash by in splendour from rout or ball,
Statesmen grown weary with long debate,

Hurry by homewards, and fling him alms;
Pitiful women, touched by the psalms,
Bringing back innocence, stoop by the wall
Where he sits at Dives' gate.

What are his thoughts of, stranded there?
While life ebbs and flows by, again and again,
Does the old sad Problem vex his poor brain?
" Why is the world so pleasant and fair,
Why, am I only who did no wrong
Crippled and bent out of human form?
Why are other men tall and strong?
Surely if all men were made to rejoice,
Seeing that we come without will or choice,
It were better to crawl for a day like a worm,
Than to lie like this so long!

" The blind shuffles by with a tap of his staff,
The tired tramp plods to the workhouse ward,—
But he carries his broad back as straight as a lord.
And the blind man can hear his little ones laugh,
While I lie here like a weed on the sand,
With these crooked limbs, paining me night and day

Is it true, what they tell of a far-off land,
In the sweet old faith which was preached for the poor,—
Where none shall be weary or pained any more,
Nor change shall enter nor any decay,
And the stricken down shall stand?"

And perhaps sometimes when the sky is clear,
And the stars show like lamps on the sweet summer night,
Some chance chord struck with a sudden delight,
Soars aloft with his soul, and brings Paradise near.
And then—for even nature is sometimes kind—
He lies stretched under palms with a harp of gold;
Or is whirled on by coursers as fleet as the wind ;
And is no more crippled, nor weak nor bent ;
No more painful nor impotent ;
No more hungry, nor weary nor cold,—
But of perfect form and mind.

Or may be his thoughts are of humbler cast,
For hunger and cold are real indeed ;
And he looks for the hour when his toil shall be past,
And he with sufficient for next day's need :
Some humble indulgence of food or fire,

E

Some music-hall ditty, or marvellous book,
Or whatever it be such poor souls desire ;
And with this little solace, for God would fain
Make even his measures of joy and pain,
He drones happily on in his quiet nook,
With hands that never tire.

Well, these random guesses must go for nought ;
Seeing it is wiser and easier far
To weigh to an atom the faintest star,
Than to sound the dim depths of a brother's thought.
But whenever I hear those poor snatches of song,
And see him lie maimed in body and soul,
While I am straight and healthy and strong,
I seem to redden with a secret shame,
That we should so differ who should be the same,
Till I hear their insolent chariot wheels roll
The millionaires along.

——o——

WATCH.

Oh, hark ! the languid air is still,
  The fields and woods seem hushed and dumb
But listen, and you shall hear a thrill,
  An inner voice of silence come.
Stray notes of birds, the hum of bees,
  The brook's light gossip on its way,
  Voices of children heard at play,
Leaves whispering of a coming breeze.

Oh, look ! the sea is fallen asleep,
  The sail hangs idle evermore ;
Yet refluent from the outer deep,
  The low wave sobs upon the shore.
Silent the dark cave ebbs and fills,
  Silent the broad weeds wave and sway ;
  Yet yonder fairy fringe of spray
Is born of surges vast as hills.

Oh, see ! the sky is deadly dark,
  There shines not moon nor any star ;

But gaze awhile, and you shall mark
  Some gleam of glory from afar :
Some half-hid planet's vagrant ray ;
  Some lightning flash which wakes the world ;
  Night's pirate banner slowly furled ;
And, eastward, some faint flush of day.

———o———

DROWNED.

ONLY eighteen winters old !
  Lay her with a tender hand
  On the delicate, ribbed sea-sand :
Stiff and cold ; ay, stiff and cold.

What she has been, who shall care ?
  Looking on her as she lies
  With those stony, sightless eyes,
And the sea-weed in her hair.

Think, O mothers ! how the deep
  All the dreary night did rave ;

Drowned.

Thundering foam and crested wave,
While your darlings lay asleep.

How she cleft the midnight air;
  And the idiot surge beneath
  Whirled her sea-ward to her death,
Angry that she was so fair.

Tossed her, beat her, till no more
  Rage could do, through all the night;
  Then with morning's ghastly light,
Flung her down upon the shore.

Mother! when brief years ago
  You were happy in your child,
  Smiling on her as she smiled,
Thought you she would perish so?

Man! who made her what she is;
  What, if when you falsely swore
  You would love her more and more,
You had seen her lie like this.

And, O Infinite Cause! didst Thou,
  When Thou mad'st this hapless child,

Dowered with passions, fierce and wild,
See her lie as she lies now ?

Filled with wild revolt and rage,
    All I feel I may not speak ;
    Fate so strong, and we so weak,
Like rats in a cage,—like rats in a cage.

——o——

THE WANDERING SOUL.

I REARED my virgin Soul on dainty food,
I fed her with rich fruit and garnered gold
From those fair gardens sown by pious care
    Of precious souls of old.

The long procession of the fabulous Past,
Rolled by for me—the earliest dawn of time ;
The seven great days ; the garden and the sword;
    The first red stain of crime;

The fierce rude chiefs who smote, and burned, and slew,
And all for God ; the pitiless tyrants grand,
Who piled to heaven the eternal monuments,
    Unchanged amid the sand ;

The fairy commonwealths, where Freedom first
Inspired the ready hand and glowing tongue
To a diviner art and sweeter song
    Than men have feigned or sung ;

The strong bold sway that held mankind in thrall,
Soldier and jurist marching side by side,
Till came the sure slow blight, when all the world
    Grew sick, and swooned, and died ;

Again the long dark night, when Learning dozed
Safe in her cloister, and the world without
Rang with fierce shouts of war and cries of pain,
    Base triumph, baser rout ;

Till rose a second dawn of light again,
Again the freemen stood in firm array
Behind the foss, and Pope and Kaiser came,
    Wondered and turned away ;

And then the broadening stream, till the sleek priest
Aspired to tread the path the Pagan trod,
And Rome fell once again, and the brave North
    Rose from the church to God.

All these passed by for me, till the vast tide
Grew to a sea too wide for any shore ;
Then doubt o'erspread me, and a cold disgust,
    And I would look no more.

For something said, The Past is dead and gone,
Let the dead bury their dead, why strive with Fate?
Why seek to feed the children on the husks
    Their rude forefathers ate ?

For even were the Past reflected back
As in a mirror, in the historic page,
For us its face is strange, seeing that the race
    Betters from age to age.

And if, hearing the tale we told ourselves,
We marvel how the monstrous fable grew ;
How in these far-off years shall men discern
    The fictive from the true ?

    *   *   *   *   *

Then turned I to the broad domain of Art,
To seek if haply Truth lay hidden there ;
Well knowing that of old close links connect
    The true things and the fair.

Fair forms I found, and rounded limbs divine,
The maiden's grace, the tender curves of youth,
The majesty of happy perfect years,
    But only half the truth.

For there is more, I thought, in man, and higher,
Than animal graces cunningly combined;
Since oft within the unlovely frame is set
    The shining, flawless mind.

So I grew weary of the pallid throng,
Deep-bosomed maids and stalwart heroes tall.
One type I saw, one earthy animal seal
    Of comeliness in all !

But not the awful, mystical human soul—
The soul that grovels and aspires in turn—
The soul that struggles outwards into light
    Through lips and eyes that burn.

So, from the soulless marbles, white and bare
And cold, too-perfect art, I turned and sought
The canvases, where Christian hands have left
    The fruits of holy thought.

Passion I found, and love, and godlike pain,
The swift soul rapt by mingled hopes and fears,
Eyes lit with glorious light from the Unseen,
    Or dim with sacred tears.

But everywhere around the living tree
I marked the tangled growths of fable twine,
And gross material images confuse
    The earthly and divine.

I saw the Almighty Ruler of the worlds,
The one unfailing Source of Light and Love,
A sullen gray-beard set on rolling clouds,
    Armed with the bolts of Jove.

The Eternal Son, a shapeless new-born child,
Supine upon His peasant-mother's knees,
Or else a ghastly victim, crushed and worn
    By physical agonies.

The virgin mother—now a simple girl ;
Or old and blurred with tears, and wan with sighs ;
And now a goddess, oft-times giving back
    The harlot-model's eyes.

Till faring on what spark of heaven was there,
Grew pale, then went out quite ; and in its stead,
Dull copies of dull common life usurped
    The empire of the dead.

Or if sometimes, rapt in a sweet suspense,
I knew a passionate yearning thrill my soul,
As down long aisles from lofty quires I heard
     The solemn music roll ;

Or if at last the long-drawn symphony,
After much weary wandering seemed to soar
To a finer air, and subtle measures born
     On some diviner shore,

I thought how much of poor mechanical skill,
How little fire of heart, or force of brain,
Was theirs who first devised or now declared
     That magical sweet strain ;

And how the art was partial, not immense,
As Truth is, or as Beauty, but confined
To this our later Europe, not spread out,
     Wide as the width of mind.

*   *   *   *   *

So then from Art, and all its empty shows
And outward-seeming truth, I turned and sought
The secret springs of knowledge which lie hid
     Deep in the wells of thought.

The hoary thinkers of the Past I knew ;
Whose dim vast thoughts, to too great stature grown,
Flashed round as fitful lightning flashes round
    The black vault of the Unknown.

Who, seeing that things are Many, and yet are One ;
That all things suffer change, and yet remain—
That opposite flows from opposite, Life and Death,
    Love, Hatred, Pleasure, Pain—

Raised high upon the mystical throne of life
Some dim abstraction, hopeful to unwind
The tangled maze of being, by one rude guess
    Of an untutored mind.

The sweet Ideal Essences revealed,
To that high poet-thinker's eyes I saw ;
The archetypes which underset the world
    With one broad perfect Law.

The fair fantastic Commonwealth, too fair
For earth, wherein the wise alone bore rule—
So wise that oftentimes the sage himself
    Shows duller than the fool ;

And that white soul, clothed with a satyr's form,
Which shone beneath the laurels day by day,
And, fired with burning faith in God and Right,
    Doubted men's doubts away ;

And him who took all knowledge for his own,
And with the same swift logical sword laid bare
The depths of heart and mind, the mysteries
    Of earth and sea and air ;

And those on whom the visionary East
Worked in such sort, that knowledge grew to seem
An ecstasy, a sudden blaze, revealed
    To crown the mystic's dream ;

Till, once again, the old light faded out,
And left no trace of that fair day remain—
Only a barren method, binding down
    Men's thoughts with such a chain

That knowledge sank self-slain, like some stout knight
Clogged by his harness ; nor could wit devise
Aught but ignoble quibbles, subtly mixed
    With dull theologies.

Not long I paused with these ; but passed to him
Who, stripping, like a skilful wrestler, cast
From his strong arms the precious deadly web,
    The vesture of the past.

And looked in Nature's eyes, and, foot to foot,
Strove with her daily, till the witch at length
Gave up, reluctant, to the eyes of the mind
    The secret of her strength.

And then the old fight, fought on modern fields,—
Whether we know by sense or inward sight—
Whether a law within, or use alone,
    Mark out the bounds of right.

All these were mine ; and then the ancient doubt,
Which scarce kept silence as this master taught
The undying soul, or that one subtly probed
    The process of our thought,

And shuddered at the dreadful innocent talk
To the cicala's chirp beneath the trees—
Love poised on silver wings, love fallen and fouled
    By black iniquities ;

And laughed to scorn their quest of cosmic law,
Saw folly in the mystic and the schools,
And in the newer method gleams of truth
      Obscured by childish rules;

Rose to a giant's strength, and always cried—
You shall not find the truth here, she is gone; ˙
What glimpse men had, was ages since, and these
      Go idly babbling on—

Jangles of opposite creeds, alike untrue,
Quaint puzzles, meaningless logomachies,
Efforts to pierce the infinite core of things
      With purblind finite eyes.

Go, get you gone to Nature, she is kind
To reasonable worship; she alone
Thinks scorn, when humble seekers ask for bread,
      To offer them a stone.

      *   *   *   *   *

And Nature drew me to her, and awhile
Enchained me.   Day by day, things strange and new
Rose on me; day by day, I seemed to tread
      Fresh footsteps of the true.

I laid life's house bare to its inmost room
With lens and scalpel, marked the simple cell
Which might one day be man or creeping worm,
    For aught that sense could tell,—

Thrust life to its utmost home, a speck of gray
No more nor higher, traced the wondrous plan,
The infinite wise appliances which shape
    The dwelling-place of man,—

Nor halted here, but thirsted still to know,
And, with half-blinded eyesight, loved to pore
On that scarce visible world, born of decay
    Or stranded on the shore.

Marked how the Mother works with earth and gas,
And with what subtle alchemy knows to blend
The vast conflicting forces of the world
    To one harmonious end;

And, nightly gazing on the splendid stars,
Essayed in vain with reverent eye to trace
The chain of miracles by which men learnt
    The mysteries of space;

And toiled awhile with spade and hammer, to learn
The long long sequences of life, and those
Unnumbered cycles of forgotten years
     Ere life's faint light arose ;

And loved to trace the strange sweet life of flowers,
And all the scarce suspected links which span
The gulf betwixt the fungus and the tree,
     And 'twixt the tree and man.

Then suddenly, " What is it that I know ?
I know the shows and changes, not the cause ;
I know but long successions, which usurp
     The name and rank of laws.

" And what if the design I think I see
Be but a pitiless order, through the long
Slow wear of chance and suffering working out
     Salvation for the strong ?

" How else, if scheme there be, can I explain
The cripple or the blind, the ravening jaw,
The infinite waste of life, the plague, the sword,
     The evil, thriftless law,

" Or seeming errors of design, or strange
Complexities of structure, which suggest
A will which sported with its power, or worked
    Not careful for the best ?"

I could not know the scheme, nor therefore spend
My soul in painful efforts to conform
With those who lavished life and brain to trace
    The story of a worm ;

Nor yet with those who, prizing overmuch
The unmeaning jargon of their science, sought
To hide, by arrogance, from God and man
    Their poverty of thought,

And, blind with fact and stupified by law,
Lost sight of the Creator, and became
Dull bigots, narrowed to a hopeless creed,
    And priests in all but name.

    *   *   *   *   *

Thus, tired with seeking truth, and not content
To dwell with those weak souls who love to feign
Unending problems of the life and love
    Which they can ne'er explain ;

Nor those who, parrot-like, are proud to clothe
In twenty tongues the nothing that they know;
Nor those whom barren lines and numbers blind
    To all things else below;

And half-suspecting, when the poet sang
And drew my soul to his, and round me cast
Fine cords of fancy, but a sleight of words,
    Part stolen from the past—

I thought, My life lies not with books, but men!
Surely the nobler part is his who guides
The State's great ship through hidden rocks and sands
    Rude winds and popular tides,—

A freeman amongst freemen,—and contrives,
By years of thought and labour, to withdraw
Some portion of their load from lives bent down
    By old abusive law!

A noble task; but how to walk with those
Who ever by fate's subtle irony hold
The freeman's ear—the cunning fluent knave,
    The dullard big with gold?

And how, where worthier souls bore rule, to set
The Faction higher than Truth, or stoop to cheat,
With cozening words and shallow flatteries
    The Solons of the street?

Or, failing this, to wear a hireling sword—
Ready, whate'er the cause, to kill and slay,
And float meanwhile, a gilded butterfly,
    My brief inglorious day—

Or, in the name of Justice, to confuse,
For hire, with shameless tongue and subtle brain,
Dark riddles, which, to honest minds unwarped,
    Are easy to explain—

Or, with keen salutary knife, to carve
For hire the shrinking limb ; or else to feign
Wise words and healing powers, though knowing naught
    In face of death and pain—

Or grub all day for pelf 'mid hides and oils,
Like a mole in some dark alley, to rise at last,
After dull years, to wealth and ease, when all
    The use for them is past—

Or else to range myself with those who seek
By reckless throws with chance, by trick and cheat,
Swift riches lacking all the zest of toil,
    And only bitter-sweet.

Or worst, and still for hire, to feign to hear
A voice which called not, calling me to tell
Now of an indolent heaven, and now, obscene
    Threats of a bodily hell.

   *   *   *   *   *

Then left I all, and ate the husks of sense ;
Oh, passionate coral lips ! oh, shameful fair !
Bright eyes, and ready smiles, and rounded snows!
    Oh, golden rippling hair !

Oh, rose-strewed feasts, made glad with wine and song,
And laughter-lit ! oh, whirling dances sweet,
When the mad music faints awhile and leaves
    Low beats of rhythmic feet !

Oh, glorious terrible moments, when the sheen
Of silk, and straining limbs flash thundering by,
And name and fame and honour are set upon
    Worse hazard than the die !

All these were mine.   Then, thought I, I have found
The truth at last; here comes not doubt to pain ;
Here things are what they seem, not figments, born
    Of a too busy brain.

But soon, the broken law avenged itself ;
For, oh, the pity of it ! to feel the fire
Grow colder daily, and the soaring soul
    Sunk deep in grosser mire.

And oh, the pity of it ! to drag down lives
Which had been happy else, to ruin, and waste
The precious affluence of love, which else
    Some humble home had graced.

And oh ! the weariness of feasts and wine ;
The jests where mirth was not, the nerves unstrung.
The throbbing brain, the tasteless joys, which keep
    Their savour for the young.

These came upon me, and a vague unrest,
And then a gnawing pain ; and then I fled,
As one some great destruction passes, flees
    The city of the dead.

    *   *   *   *   *

Then, pierced by some vague sense of guilt and pain ;
"God help me !" I said. "There is no help in life,
Only continual passions waging war,
  Cold doubt and endless strife!"

But He is full of peace, and truth, and rest,
I give myself to Him; I strive to find
What words divine have fallen from age to age
  Fresh from the Eternal Mind.

And so, upon the reverend page I dwelt,
Which shows Him formless, self-contained, all-wise.
Passionless, pure, the soul of visible things,
  Unseen by mortal eyes ;

Who oft across dim gulfs of time revealed,
Grew manifest, then passed and left a foul
Thick mist of sense and error to obscure
  The upward gazing soul ;

And those which told of opposite principles,
Of Light with Darkness warring evermore ;
Alas ! 'twas nothing new, I had felt the fight
  Within my soul before.

And those wise answers of the far-off sage,
So wise, they shut out God, and can enchain
To-day in narrow bonds of foolishness
    The subtle Eastern brain.

And last, the hallowed pages dear to all,
Which bring God down to earth, a King to fight
With His people's hosts; or speaking awful words
    From out the blaze of light,—

Which tell how earthly chiefs who loved the right,
Were dear to Him; and how the poet king
Sang, from his full repentant heart, the strains
    Sad hearts still love to sing.

And how the seer was filled with words of fire,
And passionate scorn and lofty hate of ill
So pure, that we who hear them seem to hear
    God speaking to us still.

But mixed with these dark tales of fraud and blood,
Like weeds in some fair garden; till I said,
"These are not His; how shall a man discern
    The living from the dead?

" I will go to that fair Life, the flower of lives ;
I will prove the infinite pity and love which shine
From each recorded word of Him who once
    Was human, yet Divine.

" Oh, pure sweet life, crowned by a godlike death ;
Oh tender healing hand ; oh words that give
Rest to the weary, solace to the sad,
    And bid the hopeless live !

" Oh pity, spurning not the penitent thief;
Oh wisdom, stooping to the little child ;
Oh infinite purity, taking thought for lives
    By sinful stains defiled !

" With thee, will I dwell, with thee." But as I mused,
Those pale ascetic words renewed my doubt :
The cheek, which to the smiter should be turned,
    The offending eye plucked out.

The sweet, impossible counsels which may seem
Too careless of the state ; nor recognise
A duty to the world, not all reserved
    For that beyond the skies.

"And was it truth, or some too reverent dream
Which scorned God's precious processes of birth,
And spurned aside for Him, the changeless laws
    Which rule all things of earth?

" Or how shall some strange breach of natural law
Be proof of moral truth ; yet how deny
That He who holds the cords of life and death
    Can raise up those who die ?

" Yet how to doubt that God may be revealed ;
Is He more strange, incarnate, shedding tears,
Than when the unaided scheme fulfils itself
    Through countless painful years ?

" But if revealed He be, how to escape
The critic who dissects the sacred page,
Till God's gift hangs on grammar, and the saint
    Is weaker than the sage !"

These warring thoughts held me, and more; but when
The simple life divine shone forth no more,
And the fair truth came veiled in stately robes
    Of philosophic lore ;

And 'twas the apostle spoke, and not the Christ ;
The scholar, not the Master ; and the Church
Defined itself, and sank to earthly thrones :
    " Surely," I said, " my search

" Is vain ; " and when with magical rite and spell
They killed the Lord, and sought with narrow creed,
Half-fancy, half of barbarous logic born,
    To heal the hearts that bleed ;

And heretic strove with heretic, and the Church
Slew for the truth itself had made : again,
" Can these things be of Him ? " I thought, and felt
    The old undying pain.

And yet the fierce false prophet turned to God
The gross idolatrous East ; and far away,
Beyond the horrible wastes, the lewd knave makes
    A paradise to-day.

      *   *   *   *   *

Yet still deep down, within my being I kept
Two sacred fires alight through all the strife, —
Faith in a living God ; faith in a soul
    Dowered with an endless life.

And therefore though the world's foundations shook,
I was not all unhappy; knowing well
That He whose hand sustained me would not bear
To leave my soul in hell.

But now I looked on nature with strange eyes,
For something whispered, " Surely all things pass ;
All life decays on earth or air or sea, —
All wither like the grass."

" These are, then have been, we ourselves decline,
And cease and turn to earth, and are as they :
Shall our dear animals rise ; shall the dead flowers
Bloom in another May ?

" The seed springs like the herb, but not the same ;
And like us, not the same, our children rise ;
.The type survives, though suffering gradual change,
The individual dies.

" How shall one seek to sever, e'en in thought,
Body and soul ; how show to doubting eyes
That this returns to dust, while the other soars
Deathless beyond the skies ?

" And if it be a lovely dream—no more,
And life is ended with our latest breath,
May not the same sweet fancy have devised
    The Lord of life and death ?

" We know Him not ; we may not e'en conceive
Beginning or yet ending.   Is it more
To image an eternal world, than one
    Where nothing was before ?

" Whence came the Maker ?   Was He uncreate ?
Then why must all things else created be ?
Was He created ?   Then, the Lord I serve,
    Lies farther off than He.

" Or if He be indeed, yet the soul dies.
Why, what is He to us ? not here, not here !
His judgments fall, wrong triumphs here—right sinks ;
    What hope have we, or fear ? "

I could not answer, yet when others came,
Affirming He was not, and bade me live
In the present only, seizing unconcerned
    What pleasures life could give,

My doubt grown fiercer, scoffed at them, " Oh fools,
And blind, your joys I know ; the universe
Confutes you; can you see right yield to might,
     The better to the worse,—

" Nor burn to adjust them ?   If it were a dream,
Would all men dream it ?   Can your thought conceive
The end you tell of better than the life,
     Which all men else believe ?

" Or if we shrink as from a hateful voice,
From mute analogies of frame and shape,
Surely no other than a breath Divine
     Gave reason to the ape."

" What made all men to call on God ? what taught
The soaring soul its lofty heavenward flight?
What made us to discern the strait bounds set,
     To sever wrong from right ?

" Be sure, no easier is it to declare
He is not than He is : " and I who sought
Firm ground, saw here the same too credulous faith
     And impotence of thought.

And when they brought me their fantastic creed,
With a figment for a god—mock ceremonies —
Man worshipping himself—mock priests to kill
    The soul's high liberties,—

I spurned the folly with a curse, and turned
To dwell with my own soul apart, and there
Found no companion but the old doubt grown
    To a horrible despair.

    *   *   *   *   *

Then, as a man who, on a sunny day,
Feeling some trifling ache, unknown before,
Goes careless from his happy home, and seeks
    A wise physician's door.

And when he comes forth, neither heeds nor sees
The joyous tide of life or smiling sky,
But always, always hears a ceaseless voice
    Repeating " Thou shalt die."

So all the world flowed by, and all my days
Passed like an empty vision, and I said,
" There is no help in life ; seeming to live,
    We are but as the dead."

And thus, I tossed about long time ; at last
Nature rebelled beneath the constant pain,
And the dull sleepless care forgot itself,
    In frenzy of the brain.

And sometimes all was blackness, unrelieved,
And sometimes I would wander day and night,
Through fiery long arcades, which seared my brain
    With flakes of blinding light.

And then I lay unmoved in a gray calm;
Not life nor death, and the past came to seem
Thought, act, faith, doubt, things of but little worth,
    A dream within a dream.

    *   *   *   *   *

But, when I saw my country like a cloud,
Sink in the East, and the free ocean wind
Fanned life's returning flame and roused again
    Slow pulse and languid mind ;

Soon the great rush and mystery of the sea,
The grisly depths, the great waves coursing on,
Dark with white spuming crests which threaten death.
    Swoop by, and so are gone.

And the strong sense of weakness, as we sped—
Tossed high, plunged low, through many a furious night,
And slept in faith, that some poor seaman woke
  To guide our course aright.

All lightened something of my load, and seemed
To solace me a little, for they taught,
That the impalpable unknown might stretch,
  E'en to the realms of thought.

And so I wandered into many lands,
And over many seas; I felt the chill
Which in mid ocean strikes on those who near
  The spire-crowned icy hill,

And threaded fairy straits beneath the palms,
Where, year by year, the tepid waters sleep ;
And where, round coral isles, the sudden sea
  Sinks its unfathomed deep.

Upon the savage feverish swamp, I trod
The desert sands, the fat low plains of the East ;
On glorious storied shores and those where man
  Was ever as the beast.

And, day by day, I felt my frozen soul,
Soothed by the healing influence of change,
' Grow softer, registering day by day,
    Things new, unknown, and strange.

Not therefore, holding what it spurned before,
Nor solving riddles, which before perplexed;
But with new springs of sympathy, no more
    By impotent musings vexed.

    *   *   *   *   *

And last of all I knew the lovely land
Which was most mighty, and is still most fair;
Where world-wide rule and heavenward faith have left
    Their traces everywhere.

And as from province to province I wandered on,
City or country, all was fair and sweet;
The air, the fields, the vines, the dark-eyed girls,
    The dim arcaded street;

The minsters lit for vespers, in the cool;
Gay bridals, solemn burials, soaring chant,
Spent in high naves, gray cross, and wayside shrine,
    And kneeling suppliant;

And painting, strong to aid the eye of faith,
And sculpture, figuring awful destinies ;
Tall campaniles, crowning lake-lit hills,
    And sea-worn palaces.

Then, as the sweet days passed me one by one,
New tides of life through body and soul were sent :
And daily sights of beauty worked a calm
    Ineffable content.

And soon, as in the spring, ere frosts are done,
Deep down in earth the black roots quicken and start,
I seemed to feel a spring of faith and love
    Stir through my frozen heart.

    *   *   *   *   *

Till one still summer eve, when as I mused
By a fair lake, from many a silvery bell,
Thrilled from thin towers, I heard the Angelus,
    Deep peace upon me fell.

And following distant organ-swells, I passed
Within the circuit of a lofty wall,
And thence within dim aisles, wherein I heard
    The low chant rise and fall.

And dark forms knelt upon the ground, and all
Was gloom, save where some dying day-beam shone,
High in the roof, or where the votive lamp
    Burned ever dimly on.

Then whether some chance sound or solemn word
Across my soul a precious influence cast,
Or whether the fair presence of a faith
    Born of so great a past,

Smote on me—lo ! the wintry days were gone,
And once again the spring-time, and once more
Faith from its roots bloomed heavenward—and I sank
    Weeping upon the floor.

    *   *   *   *   *

Long time within that peaceful home I dwelt
With those grave brethren, spending silent days
And watchful nights, in solemn reverent thought,
    Made glad by frequent praise.

And the awakened longing for the Truth,
With the great dread of what had been before,
The ordered life, the nearer view of heaven,
    Worked on me more and more.

So that, I lived their life of prayer and praise,
Alike in summer heats and wintry snows,
Pacing chill cloisters 'neath the wanin g stars,
    Long ere the slow sun rose.

And speaking little, and bringing down my soul,
With frequent fast and vigil, saw at length
Truth's face show daily clearer and more clear
    To failing bodily strength.

For living in a mystical air, and grown
Athirst for faith and truth ; at last I brought
The old too-active logic to enforce
    The current of my thought.

And wishing to believe, I took for true
The shameless subtleties which dare to tell
How the Eternal charged one hand to hold
    The keys of heaven and hell.

" For if a faith be given, then must there be
A Church to guard it, and a tongue to speak,
And an unerring mind to rule alike
    The strong souls and the weak."

" And, because God's high purpose stands not still,
But He is ever with His own, the tide '
Of miracle and dogma ceases not,
 But flows down strong and wide,

" To the world's ending." So my mind fell prone,
Before the Church; and teachings new and strange :
The wafer, which they turned into their God,
 By some incredible change—

The substance which is changed, and yet retains
The self-same accidents; the Virgin Queen,
Immaculate in birth, and without death,
 Soaring to worlds unseen—

The legends, always foolish, sometimes fair,
Of saints who set all physical laws at nought :
The miracles, the portents, not the charm,
 Of the old Pagan thought—

These shook me not at all, who only longed
To drain the healing draught of faith again,
And dreaded, with a coward's dread, the thought
 Of the old former pain.

The more incredible the tale, the more
The merit of belief; the more I sought
To reason out the truth, I knew the more
    The impotence of thought.

And thus the swift months passed in prayer and praise,
Bringing the day when those tall gates should close,
And shut me out from thought and life and all
    Our heritage of woes.

     *   *   *   *   *

Then, one day, when the end drew very near,
Which should blot out the past for ever, and I
Waited impatient, longing for the hour
    When my old self should die;

I knelt at noon, within the darkened aisles,
Before a doll tawdry with rich brocade,
And all ablaze with gems, the precious gifts
    Which pious hands had made :

Nor aught of strange I saw, so changed was I,
In that dull fetish ; nay, heaven's gate unsealed,
And the veiled angels bent before the throne,
    Where sat their Lord revealed.

While like a flood the ecstasy of faith
Surged high and higher, only to fall at last
Lower and lower, when the rapture failed
    And faded, and was past.

Lo, a sweet sunbeam, straying through the gloom
Smote me, as when the first low shaft of day
Aslant the night-clouds shoots, and momently
    Chases the mists away.

And that ideal heaven was closed, and all
That reverend house turned to a darkened room,
A den of magic, masking with close fumes
    The odours of the tomb.

    *   *   *   *   *

Then passed I forth. Again my soul was free ;
Again the summer sun and exquisite air
Made all things smile ; and life and joy and love
    Were round me everywhere.

And over all the earth there went a stir,
A movement, a renewal. Round the spring
In the broad village street, the dark-eyed girls
    Were fain to dance and sing

For the glad time.   The children played their play,
Like us who play at life ; light bursts of song
Came from the fields, and to the village church
  A bridal passed along.

Far on the endless plain, the swift steam drew
A soft white riband.   Down the lazy flow
Of the broad stream, I marked, round sylvan bends,
  The seaward barges go.

The brown vine-dresser, bent among his vines,
Ceased sometimes from his toil to hold on high
His laughing child, while his deep-bosomed wife
  Cheerful sat watching by.

And all the world was glad, and full of life,
And I grew glad with it, and quickly·came
To see my past life as it was, and feel
  A salutary shame.

For what was it I had wished?   To set aside
The perfect scheme of things, to live apart
A sterile life, divorced from light and love,
  Sole, with an empty heart.

And wherefore to fatigue the Eternal ear
With those incessant hymns of barren praise?
Does not a sweeter sound go up to Him
    From well-spent toilsome days,—

And natural life, refined by honest love,
And sweet unselfish liturgies of home,
The scheme of being, worked out by duteous souls.
    Careless of what may come?

What need has He for praise? The flowers, the woods,
The winds, the seas, the plains, the mountains, praise
Their Maker, with a grander litany
    Than our poor voices raise.

What need has He of them? And looking back
To those gray walls which late had shown so fair,
I felt as one who from a dungeon 'scapes
    To free unfettered air.

And half distrustful of myself, and full
Of terror of what might be, once more fled,
With scarce a glance behind, as one who flees
    The city of the dead.

   *   *   *   *   *

All through that day and night I journeyed on
To the northward.   With the dawn, a tender rose
Blushed in mid heaven, and looking up, I saw
      Far off, the eternal snows.

Then all day higher, higher, from the plain,
Beyond the tinkling folds, beyond the fair
Dense, self-sown chestnuts, then the scented pines,
      And then an eager air,

And then the rough paths and the nearer snows;
And ever as I climbed, I seemed to cast
My former self behind, and all the rags
      Of that unlovely past:

The doubts, the superstitions, the regrets,
The awakening; as the soul which hears the loud
Archangel summon, rising, casts behind
      Corruption and the shroud.

For I was come into a higher land,
And breathed a purer air than in the past;
And He who brought me to the dust of death
      Had holpen me at last.

            *   *   *   *   *

What then ?   A dream of sojourn 'mid the hills,
A stir of homeward travel, swift and brief,
Because the very hurry of the change
  Brought somewhat of relief.

A dream of a fair city, the chosen seat
Of all the pleasures, impotent to stay
The thirsty soul, whose water-springs were laid
  In dear lands far away.

A dream of the old crowds, the smoke, the din
Of our dear mother, dearer far than fair ;
The home of lofty souls and busy brains,
  Keener for that thick air.

Then a long interval of patient toil,
Building the gradual framework of my art,
With eyes which cared no more to seek the whole,
  Fast fixed upon the part.

And mind, which shunned the general, absorbed
In the particular only, till it saw
What boundless possibilities lie between
  The matter and the law !

How that which may be rules, not that which must ;
And absolute truth revealed, would serve to blind
The soul's bright eye, and sear with tongues of flame
    The sinews of the mind.

How in the web of life, the thread of truth
Is woven with error ; yet a vesture fair
Comes from the loom—a precious royal robe
    Fit for a god to wear.

Till at the last, upon the crest of toil
Sat Knowledge, and I gained a newer truth :
Not the pale queen of old, but a soft maid,
    Filled with a tender ruth.

And, ray by ray, the clear-faced unity
Orbed itself forth, and lo ! the noble throng
Of patient souls, who sought the truth in act,
    And grew, through silence, strong.

Till prizing union more than dissidence,
And holding high the race, I came to prove
A spring of sympathy within, which swelled
    To a deep stream of love.

And Knowledge gave me gold, and power, and fame,
And honour ; and Love, a clearer, surer view :
Thus in calm depths I moored my weary soul
    Fast anchored to the True.

   *   *   *   *   *

     *   *   *   *

And now the past lies far away, and I
Can scarce recall those vanished days again ;
No more the old faith stirs me, and no more
    Comes the old barren pain.

For now each day brings its appointed toil,
And every hour its grateful sum of care ;
And life grows sweeter, and the gracious world
    Shows day by day more fair.

For now I live a two-fold life ; my own
And yet another's ; and another heart
Which beats to mine, makes glad the lonely world
    Where once I lived apart.

And little lives are mine to keep unstained,
Strange mystic growths, which day by day expand.
Like the flowers they are, and set me in a fair
　　Perpetual wonderland.

New senses, gradual language, dawning mind,
And with each day that passes, traced more strong
On those white tablets, awful characters
　　That tell of right and wrong.

And what hand wrote them? One brief life declined,
Went from us, and is not. Ah! what and where
Is that fair soul? Surely it somewhere blooms
　　In purer, brighter air.

What took it hence, and whither? Can I bear
To think, that I shall turn to a herb, a tree,
A little earth or lime, nor care for these,
　　Whatever things may be?

Or shall the love and pity I feel for these
End here, nor find a higher type or task?
I am as God to them, bestowing more
　　Than they deserve or ask.

The Wandering Soul.

And shall I find no Father? Shall my being
Aspire in vain for ever, and always tend
To an impossible goal, which none shall reach,—
    An aim without an end?

Or, shall I heed them when they bid me take
No care for aught but what my brain may prove?
I, through whose inmost depths from birth to death,
    Strange heavenward currents move;

Vague whispers, inspirations, memories,
Sanctities, yearnings, secret questionings,
And oft amid the fullest blaze of noon,
    The rush of hidden wings?

Nay; my soul spurns it! Less it is to know
Than to have faith : not theirs who cast away
The mind God gave them, eager to adore
    Idols of baser clay.

But theirs, who marking out the bounds of mind,
And where thought rules, content to understand,
Know that beyond its kingdom lies a dread
    Immeasurable land.

A land which is, though fainter than a cloud,
Full of sweet hopes and awful destinies :
A dim land, rising when the eye is clear
    Across the trackless seas.

*   *   *   *   *

O life ! O death ! O faithful wandering soul !
O riddle of being, too hard to understand !
These are Thy dreadful secrets, Lord ; and we
    The creatures of Thy hand.

O wells of consciousness, too deep for thought,
These are Thy dwelling, awful Lord Divine ;
Thine are we still, the creatures of Thy hand,
    Living and dying, Thine.

———o———

TO A CHILD IN AUTUMN.

ONLY a handful of autumn leaves,
Withered and dead ;
Yet hardly four little months or so
Have shone, O child, on your sunny head,—
Since the woods rejoiced in their tender green,
And by the great miracle which is done,
Year by year, and so is none.
All the mighty forces unseen,
Working in silence, and blent together,
The great sun stooping to kiss the earth !
And she, grown glad for the soft spring weather,
Accomplished nature's annual birth :
And, after the winter's trouble and strife,
Came peace, and death's dry bones grew animate with life.

So by degrees the weary earth once more
Wakes and puts on her cheerful robes again,—
Yet grudgingly, as one who knew before
That life was full of pain.
So, day by day, and night by night,
Blind forces, growing hourly stronger,

Stir through the plants, the grass, the trees,
Life yearning upwards to the light,
Bears on its prison locks till they no longer
Can keep it captive; so by slow degrees,
The tender leaf unfurled
Bursts from its glossy sheath, and lo, the awakened world!

And growing stronger every day,
The flush of life coursing through every vein,
The folded leaflet hastening to obey
The hidden necessity which doth pre-ordain
What she shall be, gives to the balmy air
Strong glossy fronds of darker hue,
And rioting in the growing light, like you,
O child, and daily gaining strength,
And losing innocence, at length,
As you will, issues in a thing more fair,
Which swells within her like a hidden soul,
And bursts at last in glorious spikes of bloom,
Purple and violet-sweet.
And sheltered safe within the odorous gloom,
Birds build their nests, and bees make busy hum;
Through the sweet night the grave-eyed planets roll,

And the swift hours trip by with lightsome feet;
And one by one the charms of life's young summer come.

Till comes the time when nature seems to halt,
Tired of her task, and longing it were done.
And day by day the unchanging, tyrannous sun,
Waxes and wanes; and 'neath his fierce assault,
All tender graces vanish, all the flowers
Are gone, and weeds grow rank, and every nest
Is empty, and the woods are mute from song.
And in the leafy bowers
Foul creatures writhe and prey in fierce unrest,
Like hidden thoughts of wrong;
And little carking jaws begin to wear
The glossy surfaces, which here and there
Wither and curl with rust.
And all the earth lies sunk in dull content;
And all the languid air is full of dust;
And nature like a weary toiler spent
In this her sultry afternoon of life,
Stagnates in weary pomp and soulless glare,
Yet reaps she nought as yet from all her care;
And slothful languor, masking secret strife,

Only a sordid hour,
Without the fruits of age, or youth's sweet purple flower.

And so at length, with the fading year,
There comes a tender time once more,
When the golden corn is gathered in,
And orchards blush with their ruddy store ,
And the creeping things have slunk away,
And the sun shines soberly every day ;
And the nights are cool and calm and bright ;
And the year clings more fondly to life and light,
Now that its labour is over and done.
And the woods grow glorious with purple and red,
As bright as the flowers of Spring ;
And silver gossamers float over head,
And birds half-doubting begin to sing
Low songs of deep regret.
Sweeter than love, and leaves of tender green,
Sprinkled among the russet glades are seen,
Yet by the twilight cold,
The mists, the fading light, the morning's rime ;
We know the coming of the sad sweet time,
When like the life of man the weary year grows old.

Then one by one they tremble down,
The tender leaves of Spring; and there
Lie round the bare trunks, sere and brown,
They that were once so fair.
Or, it may be, a great wind, rude and high,
Scatters and whirls them 'twixt earth and sky,
Till they wander far away.
Yet they sink at last to the bounteous earth,
And rest on her bosom who gave them birth;
And when the increasing day
Brings back the throb of Spring-time again,
Fresh leaves shall come to clothe the trees,
Larger and greener, for those that are gone.
For, ever by such dark ways as these,
Life springing from death, and joy from pain,
The eternal chariot-wheels roll grandly on;
And the great Husbandman, who prizes mould
Higher than solid gold,
Works out His hidden will; so you O child
In whom life's current courses strong and wild,
Learn, looking on these lives grown sere and brown,
What end awaits our own.
Nor therefore sorrow; for though body and mind

May seem to perish, whether ripe decay
Wither our Saxon race, or some rude wind
Sent over seas, or venomous civil broil ;
Yet not in vain has been the accomplished toil,
But man grows richer for it. It may be,
That all our ancient types shall suffer change,
And all our stately forests sway and fall ;
And some new form shall issue, vast and strange,
In ·those great fields beyond the Western sea :
Who knows?   Yet man is richer for it all.
And so in time, God willing, the great tree
Of which we are but leaves, shall wax and grow
In such brave sort, that it from sea to sea
May stretch its boughs, and send its roots so low
To the central earth, and lift its head so high
Above earth's vapours to the unclouded sky,
That increase and decay
Shall cease, and Life at last shine with a constant Day.

THE WEARY RIVER.

THERE is a ceaseless river,
    Which flows down evermore
Into a wailing ocean,
    A sea without a shore.

Broken by laughing ripple,
    Foaming with angry swell,
Sweet music as of heaven,
    Deep thunder as of hell.

Gay fleets float down upon it,
    And sad wrecks, full of pain :
But all alike it hurries
    To that unchanging main.

Sometimes 'tis foul and troubled,
    And sometimes clear and pure ;
But still the river flows, and still
    The dull sea doth endure.

And thus 'twill flow for ever,
    Till time shall cease to be :
O weary, weary river,
    O bitter, barren sea.

MARTYRS.

AH life has still its martyrs, great as those
Who bore the horrible despite of men,
The cruel rack to tear the willing limbs,
The ravening lions, or the fiery stake.
Think ye they knew a deeper pain, O friends,
Than theirs, who live with one great void unfilled,
Who, sickening through the waste of weary years,
Cherish a secret yearning, such as theirs
Who bear a hidden love, themselves unloved?
The maiden tricked to barren maidenhood;
The man who merits fame, yet finds it not;
The mother weeping for an only child,
Dead after years of longing; the good wife
Chained to the sensual churl; the gentle lady
Forced in the evening of her days to toil,
Deserted of her children, or to eat
The bitter bread of alms,—think ye that these
Suffer a lighter pain than those who went
Joyful to that brief agony? But an hour
And they should reign with Christ.

But those who bear
Through lingering years a life-long gnawing pain,

And bear without a murmur,—shall not God
Accept their gentler worship ? Shall He give them
A duller glory, or a lower crown ?

————o————

TRUTH IN FALSEHOOD.

Your little hand in mine I rest :
   The slender fingers, white and long,
   Lie in my broad palm, rude and strong,
Like birdlings in their nest.

Yours, like yourself, so soft and white,
   So delicately free from soil ;
   Mine sunbrowned, hard with moil and toil,
And seamed with scars of fight.

Dear love ! sometimes your innocence
   Strikes me with sudden chills of fear ;
   What if you saw before you, dear,
The secret gulfs of sense ?—

The coarseness, the deceit, the sin,
　We know, who 'mid the sordid crowd
　Must press, nor midst the tumult loud
Can hear the voice within ?

What if you saw me with the eyes
　Of others,—nay, my own,—or heard
　The unworthy tale, the biting word,
The sneer that worldlings prize ?

Or knew me as I am indeed,
　No hero free from blot or stain,
　But a poor soul who drags his chain
With halting feet that bleed,—

Who oft-time slips and falls, content,
　Though bruised and weary, faint and worn,
　He toils all night, if with the morn
When life and strength are spent,

He sees some far off struggling ray,
　Dispel the palpable obscure,
　And on the eastern hills, the pure
White footprints of the day ?

But you, oh love, can never know
    These darkling paths ; for you the light
    Shines always changeless, always bright,
The self-same tempered glow.

And love with innocence combined
    The nunnery of your heart shall guard,
    And faith with eye unfailing ward
The jewel of your mind.

So be it : I would sooner be
    Steeped to the lips in lie and cheat,
    A very monster of deceit,
Than bare myself to thee.

Nay, rather would I dare to hear
    At that great day from lips of flame,
    Blown to all souls my tale of shame,
Than whispered in thine ear.

Strange riddle, to those who never knew
    Of good with evil intertwined—
    The twofold self, the links that bind
The false things to the true ;

But to the seeing eye more clear
  Than blaze of noonday.   So be sure
  If my stained life might keep thine pure,
I'd glory in it, dear.

————o————

FROM PRISON.

I HATE the narrow, sunless wall
  Which, like a cold snake, girdles round
The cloistered convent fair, and tall ;
  But blind of sight and dumb of sound,
The prison house so trim and gray,
Where life is only to obey.

I hate the blank cell, bare and white,
  Whose dull walls always coldly stare
With one dead aspect day and night,
  And even in deepest sleep are there.
The tortured figure, with bowed head,
Nailed to the cross above my bed,

Whose sad eyes, full of sorrow, seem
　To gaze reproachful night and day,
Till, waking from some hopeless dream,
　I see them with the dawning gray
Bend on me still, and always look
Sad love and pitiful rebuke.

But, most of all, I hate the long
　Monotonous litanies of praise,
The solemn mass, the weary song
　Sung in sad dawns and dreary days,
The altars tricked with gold and gem,
The Virgin with her diadem.

The Virgin! What, and must I shame,—
　I, who am lost and useless here,—
The honour of my mother's name,
　The home affections pure and dear?
Surely she knew, proved, understood,
More than the pains of motherhood!

And He, her Son. Sometimes I think,—
　God help me!—that the pain He bore;

Was no more bitter cup to drink,
 Than this dull life of yearning sore ;
His pain was brief, He left His throne
A little while to save His own.

But we, what do we here, who give
 Our barren lives through weary years
To make a lifeless dogma live,
 And keep its poor life green with tears ?
God gave the loving woman's heart :
Man bids her live, unloved, apart.

Often from out the streets below,
 To the gray church which lies outside,
I see the blithe procession go ;
 The bridegroom with the happy bride,
Fresh children's faces fair and bright,
Girl-mothers, baring bosoms white.

And 1 am young and fair as they,
 Only a girl in age as yet,
Though painful years have crept away
 Since that sad day I ne'er forget,

When all my life was closed and done,
Almost before it was begun.

Closed? Nay, but years may come and go,
  And take all youth and hope away;
But not this load of life.   Ah, no;
  Still shall I sicken as I pray,
And wear and waste as I do now,
Still fettered by a hateful vow,

Till comes the end, and I shall lie
  At rest beneath the chapel wall.
God! if I heard the secret sigh,
  The tearful voices rise and fall
From hearts like mine, unfilled, unblest,
Not heaven itself could give me rest.

But far away lies heaven, and fate
  Broods near to prison heart and mind.
I saw the dear face at the gate,
  I heard the old voice sweet and kind.
They lied; but naught can now remove
The bars which make it sin to love.

Yes, life is death, and love is sin;
   Only a pallid ghost is left—
A shadow of the fire within,
   Of warmth and tenderness bereft,—
A thrill, a faint erotic flame,
Which plays around the holy name.

Oh monstrous tissue of deceit!
   Oh blasphemy of God and love !
One day, the parted souls shall meet;
   One day, the frozen waters move.
Shine forth, great Sun of Truth ! The sky
Is blinded; help us, or we die.

———o———

TWO VOYAGES.

Two ships which meet upon the ocean waste,
And stay a little while, and interchange
Tidings from two strange lands, which lie beneath
Each its own heaven and particular stars,

And fain would tarry; but the impatient surge
Calls, and a cold wind from the setting sun
Divides them, and they sadly drift apart,
And fade, and sink, and vanish, 'neath the verge—

One to the breathless plains and treacherous seas
Smitten by the tyrannous Sun, where mind alone
Withers amid the bounteous outer-world,
And prodigal Nature dwarfs and chains the man—

One to cold rains, rude winds, and hungry waves
Spilt on the frowning granite, niggard suns,
And snows and mists which starve the vine and palm,
But nourish to more glorious growth the man.

One to the scentless flowers and songless birds,
Swift storms and poison stings and ravening jaws:
One to spring violets and nightingales,
Sleek-coated kine and honest gray-eyed skies.

One to lie helpless on the stagnant sea,
Or sink in sleep beneath the hurricane:
One to speed on, white-winged, through summer airs,
Or sow the rocks with ruin—who shall tell?

So with two souls which meet on life's broad deep,
And cling together but may not stay ; for Time
And Age and chills of Absence wear the links
Which bind them, and they part for evermore—

One to the tropic lands of fame and gold,
And feverish thirst and weariness of soul ;
One to long struggles and a wintry life,
Decked with one sweet white bloom of happy love.

For each, one fate, to live and die apart,
Save for some passing smile of kindred souls ;
Then drift away alone, on opposite tides,
To one dark harbour and invisible goal.

———o———

THE WISE RULE.

" TIME flies too fast, too fast our life decays."
    Ah, faithless ! in the present lies our being ;
And not in lingering love for vanished days !

"Come, happy future, when my soul shall live."
Ah, fool! thy life is now, and not again ;
The future holds not joy nor pain to give!

"Live for what is : future and past are naught."
Ah, blind ! a flash, and what shall be, has been.
Where, then, is that for which thou takest thought?

Not in what has been, is, or is to be,
The wise soul lives, but in a wider time,
Which is not any, but contains the three !

——o——

THE VOICE OF ONE CRYING.

CRY, cry aloud in the land, cry aloud in the streets of the
city ;
Cry and proclaim that no more shall the blood of the
people be shed.
Too long have the great ones waxed strong, without
any justice or pity,

Too long have they ground down the poor, and eaten
    the people as bread.
      Thus said the voice from the dead.

Terrible voice, I said, immoderate, voice of unreason,
Not of themselves do the lowly ones mourn, or the great
    ones rejoice ;
He who hath made them unequal, hath made all things
    in their season ;
If they are mighty and strong, they were made without
    freedom or choice.
      Cry, cry aloud, said the voice.

How shall the sins of the few be reckoned against the
    many ?
Are there no tender hearts and kind 'midst the selfish
    and proud ;
Merciful souls and pure, full of love for their suffering
    brothers ;
Pitiful, touched with compassion and care for the
    desolate crowd ?
      Cry, said the voice, cry aloud.

Nay, but the world is ruled by merciless rules unbending;

The feeble folk fade from the earth, and only the mighty
remain ;

Not men alone, but all things send upwards a clamour
unending ;

Always the whole creation travails in sorrow and pain.

Cry, said the voice, cry again.

Are not our sins and our fathers' worked out in our
children's sorrow ?

Does not excess of laughter sink at its close in a sigh ?

Mirth and enjoyment to-day turn to pain and repentance
to-morrow ;

Thousands are born every hour, in the place of the
thousands who die.

Cry, said the stubborn voice, cry.

Lo! He hath made all things ; good and evil, sorrow and
pleasure ;

Not as your ways are His ways, yet are ye not all in His
hand ?

Just is He, though ye know not the measure wherewith
He will measure ;

Dark things shall one day be clear; to obey is to understand !
  Thus that voice, solemn and grand.

————o————

OTHER DAYS.

O THRUSH, your song is passing sweet,
  But never a song that you have sung
Is half so sweet as thrushes sang
  When my dear love and I were young.

O Roses, you are sweet and red,
  Yet not so red nor sweet as were
The roses that my mistress loved
  To bind within her flowing hair.

Time filches fragrance from the flower ;
  Time steals the sweetness from the song ;
Love only scorns the tyrant's touch,
  And with the growing years grows strong.

————o————

THE TRUE MAN.

TAKE thou no thought for aught save right and truth,
Life holds for finer souls no equal prize ;
Honours and wealth are baubles to the wise,
And pleasure flies on swifter wing than youth.
If in thy heart thou bearest seeds of hell,
Though all men smile, yet what shall be thy gain ?
Though all men frown, if truth and right remain,
Take thou no thought for aught ; for it is well.

Take thou no thought for aught ; nor deem it shame
To lag behind while knaves and dullards rise ;
Thy soul asks higher guerdon, purer fame,
Than to loom large and grand in vulgar eyes.
Though thou shouldst live thy life in vile estate,
Silent, yet knowing that deep within thy breast
Unkindled sparks of genius lie repressed,—
Greater is he who is, than seemeth, great.

If thou shouldst spend long years of hope deferred,
Chilled through with doubt, and sickening to despair ;
If as cares thicken friends grow cold and rare,
Nor favouring voice in all the throng be heard ;

If all men praise him whom thou know'st to be
Of lower aims and duller brain than thine,—
Take thou no thought, though all men else combine
In thy despite : their praise is naught to thee.

Bethink thee of the irony of fate,
How great men die inglorious and alone ;
How Dives sits within upon his throne,
While good men crouch with Lazarus at the gate.
Our tree of life set on Time's hither shore
Blooms like the secular aloe once an age :
The great names scattered on the historic page
Are few indeed, but the unknown are more.

Waste is the rule of life : the gay flowers spring,
The fat fruits drop, upon the untrodden plain ;
Sea-sands at ebb are silvered o'er with pain ;
The fierce rain beats and mars the feeble wing ;
Fair forms grow fairer still for deep disease ;
Hearts made to bless are spent apart, alone.
What claim hast thou to joy, while others moan ?
God made us all, and art thou more than these ?

Take thou no care for aught save truth and right ;
Content, if such thy fate, to die obscure ;
Wealth palls and honours, Fame may not endure,
And loftier souls soon weary of delight.
Keep innocence ; be all a true man ought ;
Let neither pleasures tempt, nor pains appal :
Who hath this, he hath all things, having naught ;
Who hath it not, hath nothing, having all.

———o———

PASSING.

To spring, to bloom, to fade,—
This is the sum of the laborious years ;
Life preludes death as laughter ends in tears :
All things that God has made
Suffer perpetual change, and may not long endure.

We alter day by day ;
Each little moment, as life's current rolls,
Stamps some faint impress on our yielding souls ;
We may not rest nor stay,
Drifting on tides unseen to one dread goal and sure.

Our being is compassed round
With miracles ; on this our life-long sleep,
Strange whispers rise from the surrounding deep,
    Like that weird ocean sound
Borne in still summer nights on weary watching ears.

    The selves we leave behind
Affright us like the ghosts of friends long dead ;
The old love vanished in the present dread,
    They visit us to find
New sorrows, alien hopes, strange pleasures, other fears.

——o——

A VISION OF LOVE—DEAD.

A DREAM was mine one summer night,
Which stayed my pulses with affright ;
For that I heard a cold voice say
    "Love is dead !"
Dead, departed, fled away !
      Dead !

In that strange dream I seemed to be
Stretched on a soft slope by the sea,
Sheltered by odorous citron trees;
Above, a rosy sunlit hill,
From which a musical stream at will
Strayed through the gray-green olive wood;
Beneath, the gleaming marble stood
Of a fair temple, dedicate
To Aphrodite, amorous.
Before me, feathering with the breeze,
The blue waves curled, and fell in foam
Upon the smooth shore, clamorous:
And each one carolling to his mate,
The blithe birds sang; the lawn's soft green
Was lit with white procession
Of youths and maids, with dance and song,
Speeding to make confession
Of love to Aphrodite's ear:
Where in her shrine, beyond the long
Loud colonnade, she made her home,
On her fair throne a smiling queen,
With mischievous Eros near.

*   *   *   *   *

Then suddenly I heard a wailing voice
Proclaiming, "Love is dead;" and instantly,
The unclouded azure faded from the sea,
And left it cold and gray.   An icy wind
Swept downwards from the misty hill, and made.
Where the sun shone before, a deadly shade;
And all the thick leaves shuddered as it passed;
The crisp waves swelled to surges in the blast;
    The sweet brook fell in thunder;
Nor might they any more rejoice,
Who danced and sang with joyous mind;
    But rudely torn asunder,
Each stern youth parted from his sullen bride.
Loud angry voices rose, and women's sighs,
And words of jealous rage, and piteous cries;
Arms clashed; and, before long, the thick red rain
Stained the white pavement with the old foul stain,
And cries of pain arose on every side.
    Great kites swooped down and tore
    The tender doves, and bore
Aloft the quivering wretches, dabbled with blood.
And just before my eyes, a white-winged boat
No longer on the monstrous waves could float,

But sank, with all hands, in the furious flood.
Pain and death and mortal strife,
Where all before was love and life !

And in the inner shrine
Where shone before the gracious face divine
Of Aphrodite, mother of all,
Down the long colonnade,
Strange gibbering sounds were made,
As of black demons loosed from hell.
And in the dim, uncertain light,
Winged things obscene fluttered and shrieked in fright,
And struck against each other, and shrieking fell ;
And behind each shadowy column,
Strange spectres lurking solemn,
Threatened ; and on the darkling throne,
Not the deep-bosomed rounded grace
Of the sweet goddess of the place,
But a fierce gorgon, gaunt and still,
With snake-wreathed hair, and eyes to chill
The gazer into stone.

Nor yet with other minds or things alone
That deadly voice made havoc ; for I knew

A chill of doubt within, which grew and grew,

Till heart and brain and will seemed turned to stone.

I loathed to think, yet might I not refrain

From endless subtleties of thought, which still

Slipped from my grasp, like writhing snakes, until

    They left a sting of pain.

All causes stood effectless,—all effect

Divorced from cause ; no progress nor decay,

But an inane succession, which might tend

No whither, and yet which might not pause nor stay,

Though it had neither starting-point nor end.

So the sweet blooms with which our life is decked,

Art's tender forms, the passionate voice of song ;

Because they bore within them some faint trace

Of an ideal loveliness and grace,

Grew hateful to me.   Bounds of right and wrong

I knew to be vain juggles of words ; for how,

Since there was neither scheme, nor any plan,

But only this one act a little before,

And that one after,—how could finite man,

The thing that sleeps and wakes and is no more,

Hope to soar up beyond himself, and know

The vast periphery, of which he sees

Only an infinite arch ! And so I came
To look on honour as an empty name ;
Affection as the common bond which binds,
Each for its selfish ends, repugnant minds ;
The dead love but a corporal appetite ;
And all our faint blind motions towards the light,
Only as the moth's which flutters round and round
The flame which blinds and burns it. So at last
I loathed the thought of God ; for if when cause
Is linked to consequence by changeless laws,
There seems no room for Him in all the chain ;
Much more when neither thought nor fact are bound,
To thought or fact, but sole and isolate
Or joined by blind chance simulating fate
Are for a little while, and then are past ;
Or if He were, I loathed Him for that He,
Ruling all things, had willed them so to be.
And then I loathed myself, because I lay
Like some bark helpless on a tropic sea,
Moved by no breath of wind, but day by day
Doomed to lie rotting, till I ceased to be,
But impotent to change. And so at length,
My deep despair grown to a giant's strength,

K

I said, I will break through these chains, and try
Whether some other world beyond the sky,
Or nothingness itself, may prove more kind.
But even as thus I mused, I came to find
Some inborn blight which served to paralyse
My powerless will; nor might my thought devise
End or relief to that eternal pain,
For ever and for ever.   Then I said,
Groaning, "Ah, this it is, that love is dead !
The world has lost its soul, if love be dead :
It is the deepest hell where love is dead,
And I must bear it.
                          Then in deep affright
I woke with a start, and lo ! the dawn made bright
The gold upon my darling's sunny head.

———o———

FETTERS.

Oh who shall say that we are free !
    Surely life's chains are strong to bind,
From youth to age, from birth to death,
    Body and mind.

We run the riotous race of youth,
  Then turn from evil things to good:
'Tis but a slower pulse, a chill
  Of youth's hot blood.

We mount the difficult steeps of thought,
  Or pace the dusty paths of gain :
'Tis but that sense receding leaves
  A keener brain.

Time takes this too, and then we turn
  Our dim eyes to the hidden shore ;
Life palls, and yet we long to live,—
  Ay, nothing more.

———o———

IN MEMORY.

CLOSE, kind hand, the aged eyes ;
  Smooth the scanty locks of snow :
No more need for sobs or sighs,
  Broken words or tears of woe.

All her mortal work is done,
All the immortal has begun.

Strange ! it was but yesternight
    She was with us whom we weep ;
Yet before the tardy light,
    Waking from this lifelong sleep,
She unclosed her weary eyes
To the dawn of Paradise.

With us only yesternight !
    Planning little schemes together,—
How to make our garden bright
    In the bountiful Spring weather ;
Or with grave abstracted look
Buried in some simple book.

Only gifted yesternight
    With the logic of the heart,
Dowered to day with clearer sight
    Than our poor wisdom can impart ;
Viewing with an eye serene
What nor king nor seer hath seen.

But a loving woman then,
   Ranged among the angels now ;
Homely then in face and mien,
   Now with God's light on her brow.
With her last convulsive breath,
She shook off the bonds of death.

Mighty change ! which doth appal
   Love when one we cherish dies.
Ere the weary eyelids fall,
   Lo ! an angel's awful eyes :
Ere the languid hand grows cold,
'Tis an angel's that we hold.

Awful mystery, unseen,
   Rising round us as we tread !
Dreadful gulf that yawns between
   Us and our belovèd dead !
We like footsteps in the sand ;
They so calm, and wise, and grand.

Patience, soul ! a little space
   We shall be as wise as they ;

Swift from out its orient place
  Climbs the chariot of the day;
  See, the east is all aglow!
When that sun sinks we shall go.

———o———

LOVE'S RENEWAL.

I CHARGE you insatiate Death,
By the sacred name which no tongue may tell,
By the formless invisible world, by all
  Good angels and fiends of hell,
By all the dark charms, all the magical words,
Which seer and mystic in every land,
In monkish cloister, on desert sand,
Have muttered at midnight to ghastly shades,
  Give back my love. .

But should she come back golden-haired,
With the deep blue eyes, and the girlish grace,
With the ringing innocent laughter of old,
  And no shadow of time on her face,
And find, not the generous boy of old time,

But a broken man with his body bent,
Bankrupt of faith, and with hope long spent,
Gray, heavy-eyed, seared by the world and by age,
  Should we still love?

 Yet would I not change even a line
Of the mind or the form of that vanished day.
Could I bear to mark the shy soul in her eyes
 Wax fainter, and die away
In the haughty stare of a prosperous dame,
Or even in anxious motherly care?
I crave not the noontide's luminous air,
But the dew and the freshness of early morn,
  When life was love.

 Would I then strip from my soul
The long past's fruitage of golden grain?
Unlearn the lesson of years, and know
 Dim passionate hopes again?
Ascend without hope through the rocks and snows,
The dull path once traversed with hopeful feet,
Till the mists blot out life like a winding sheet?
Flush again with fond dreams that can no more deceive?
  Nay, not for love!

Alas ! that we are so mutable :
Poor thralls of circumstance, weakly and base.
The brute Earth changes not at all,
The dead suns roll through space ;
But for us, the eternal, who cannot die,
For us who are one with the Lord of Things,
A few dull beats of Time's pitiless wings,
And life's flame flickers and faints, and is lost,—
And with it love.

Wherefore I charge you, good Death,
Make a full end, draw near and restore
The dreams, the illusions, the haze of gold,
The hopes that are no more ;
Not here, not here, but in some dim world
Where the air is too light for Time's wings to move on,
And Past and Future are vanished and gone,
And the Infinite Present, not waxing nor waning,
Gives back my love.

—— o ——

RICH AND WISE.

WILD flowers in spring were sweet to childish hands
  As riches to the wretch possessing naught;
And as the water-springs in desert lands
  Are the pale victories of patient thought:
But sweeter, dearest, sweeter far,
The hours when we together are.

No more I know the childish joys of old,
  Nor yet have learnt the grave delights of age :
A miser, gloat I on thy locks' rich gold;
  A student, ponder on thy soul's fair page.
Thus do I grow both rich and wise,
On these fair locks and those deep eyes.

Therefore in wit and wealth do I increase,
  Poring on thee, as on a fair writ book;
No panic-fear can make that rich stream cease,
  Nor doubts confuse the crystal of thy look.
Some to the mart or to the oratory
May turn them : thou art both to me.

THE YOUNG MOTHER.

Dear heart ! what a little time it is since Francis and I
    used to walk
From church in the still June evenings together, busy
    with loving talk ;
And now he is gone, far away over seas, to some strange
    foreign country,—and I
Shall never rise from my bed any more, till the day when
    I come to die.

I tried not to think of him during the prayers ; but when
    his dear voice I heard,
I failed to take part in the hymn ; for my heart fluttered
    up to my throat like a bird,
And scarcely a word of the sermon I caught.   I doubt
    'twas a grievous sin ;
But 'twas only one poor little hour in the week that I
    had to be happy in.

When the blessing was given, and we left the dim aisles for
    the light of the evening star ;
Though I durst not lift up my eyes from the ground, yet
    I knew that he was not far.

And I hurried on, though I fain would have stayed, till I
heard his footstep draw near ;
And love rising up in my breast like a flame, cast out
every shadow of fear.

Ah me ! 'twas a pleasant pathway home,—a pleasant
pathway and sweet ;
Ankle deep through the purple clover, breast high 'mid
the blossoming wheat ;
I can hear the landrails prate through the dew, and the
night-jars' tremulous thrill,
And the nightingale pouring her passionate song from the
hawthorn under the hill.

One day, when we came to the wicket gate, 'neath the
elms, where we used to part,
His voice began to falter and break as he told me I had
his heart.
And I whispered back that mine was his : we knew what
we felt long ago ;
Six weeks are as long as a lifetime almost, when you
love each other so.

So we put up the banns, and were man and wife, in the
sweet fading time of the year,
And till Christmas was over and past, I knew no shadow
of sorrow or fear.
It seems like a dream already, alas! a sweet dream
vanished and gone,
So hurried and brief while passing away, so long to look
back upon.

I had only had him three little months, and the world
lay frozen and dead,
When the summons came, which we feared and hoped,
and he sailed over seas for our bread.
Ah, well! it is fine to be wealthy and grand, and never
to need to part ;
But 'tis better far to love and be poor, than be rich with
an empty heart.

Though I thought 'twould have killed me to lose him at
first, yet was he not going for me ?
So I hid deep down in my breast all the grief, which I
knew it would pain him to see.

He'd surely be back by the autumn, he said; and since
    his last passionate kiss,
He has scarcely been out of my thoughts, day or night,
    for a moment, from that day to this.

When I wrote to him how I thought it would be, and he
    answered so full of love,
Ah! there was not an angel happier than I, in all the
    white chorus above.
And I seemed to be lonely no longer, the days and the
    weeks passed so swiftly away;
And the March winds died, and the sweet April showers
    gave place to the blossoms of May.

And then came the sad summer-eve, when I sat with the
    little frock in the sun,
And Janet ran in with the news of the ship—Ah, well!
    may His will be done.
They said that all hands were lost, and I swooned away
    on the floor like a stone;
And another life came, ere I knew he was safe, and my
    own was over and gone.

    *   *   *   *   *   *

And now I lie helpless here, and shall never rise up
    again ;

I grow weaker and weaker, day by day, till my weakness
    itself is a pain.

Every morning the creeping dawn ; every evening I see
    from my bed

The orange-gold fade into lifeless gray, and the old
    evening star overhead.

Sometimes by the twilight dim, or the awful birth of the
    day,

As I lie, very still, not asleep nor awake, my soul seems
    to flutter away ;

And I float far beyond the stars, till I thrill with a rap-
    turous pain,

And the feeble touch of a tiny hand recalls me to life
    again.

And the doctor says she will live. Ah ! 'tis hard to leave
    her alone,

And to think she will never know, in the world, the love
    of the mother who's gone.

They will tell her of me, by-and-by, and perhaps she will
shed me a tear;
But if I should stoop to her bed in the night, she would
start with a horrible fear.

She will grow into girlhood, I trust, and will bask in the
light of love,
And I, if I gain to see her at all, shall only look on from
above.
I shall see her and cannot aid, though she fall into evil
and woe.
Ah, how can the angels find heart to rejoice, when they
think of their dear ones below?

And Francis, he too will forget me, and go on the journey
of life ;
And I hope, though I dare not think of it yet, will take
him another wife—
It will hardly be Janet, I think, though she liked him in
days gone by.
Was that why she came? But what thoughts are these
for one who is soon to die?

I hope he will come ere I go, though I feel no longer the
    thirst
For the sound of his voice and the light of his eye, which
    I used to feel at first.
'Tis not that I care for him less, but death dries, with a
    finger of fire,
The tender springs of innocent love and the torrents of
    strong desire.

And I know we shall meet again. I have done many
    things that are wrong,
But surely the Lord of Life and of Love cannot bear to
    be angry long.
I am only a girl of eighteen, and have had no teacher
    but love ;
And, it may be, the sorrow and pain I have known will
    be counted for me above.

For I doubt if the minister knows all the depths of the
    goodness of God,
When he says, He is jealous of earthly love, and bids me
    bow down 'neath the rod.

He is learnèd and wise I know, but somehow to dying
eyes
God opens the secret doors of the shrine that are closed
to the learnèd and wise.

So now I am ready to go, for I know He will do what is
best,
Though He call me away while the sun is on high, like
a child sent early to rest.
I should like him to see her first, though the yearning is
over and past :
But what is that footstep upon the stair? Oh, my
darling at last, at last !

———o———

DEAR LITTLE HAND.

DEAR little hand that clasps my own,
Embrowned with toil and seamed with strife ;
Pink little fingers not yet grown
To the poor strength of after-life, —
Dear little hand!

I.

Dear little eyes which smile on mine
  With the first peep of morning light;
Now April-wet with tears, or fine
  With dews of pity, or laughing bright.
    Dear little eyes!

Dear little voice, whose broken speech
  All eloquent utterance can transcend ;
Sweet childish wisdom strong to reach
  A holier deep than love or friend :
    Dear little voice!

Dear little life! my care to keep
  From every spot and stain of sin ;
Sweet soul foredoomed, for joy or pain,
  To struggle and—which? to fall or win?
    Dread mystical life !

———o———

I WILL ARISE.

Who, toiling on the weary round of life,
But feels sometimes,—when all the way is dark,
And mists of sense and clouds of weariness

Close round him, and before him stretches out
Life's journey, an interminable moor,
And all the future like a barren road
Through the long waste of years,—lo, suddenly
The mists rise like a curtain, and he knows
The presence of the everlasting hills.
Height after height, peak after peak, revealed ;
The filmy downward cataract, the chill
Unearthly whiteness of untrodden snows ;
And somewhere in the space 'twixt them and heaven
The eagle circling sunward ! So his soul
Knows it must quit the smooth ignoble paths,
To tread on rugged heights, scale precipices,
Sway on the trembling bridge which spans the foam,
Creep where the thund'rous avalanche sweeps, the bolt
Shivers the patient rocks, feel the mad winds
Rush round him like a chaos. If he know
Something of new-born joy, yet is it dashed
With craven chills of fear ; fain would he climb,
But looking upward dare not. Then perchance
Shines out, athwart the gathered clouds of sense
The great sun's awful face ; and lo, the snows
Which erewhile showed so cold, so deadly calm,

Redden with a blush of life : the light reveals,
High on the scarpèd cliffs, the giddy paths
Where men have trodden and lived.   Then his whole soul
Stirred to the deeps of passionate utterance,
Cries loud, "I will arise, I will arise ;"
And while the sun shines, climbs.   Happy are they
On whom the clouds descend not to blot out
What glimpse they had of heaven.   Some men there be
Who, toiling through the mist, ne'er see the sun,
And live a slavish life and know it not,
And die, poor souls! i' the plain.   Others there be
Who, when in some chance ray they fain would rise,
The envious clouds shut out the face of heaven,
And they may mount no higher.   Fewer still
Girding their loins, without a glance behind,
Mount ever upward in that mystical light,
Above the earth's gross humours, till the air
Grows purer, and the paths which seemed so steep,
Are smoothed before them and they tread the snows,
Where other footsteps few and rare shall come
In the efflux of the ages—storm and cloud
Left far beneath ; God shining overhead ;
And round them all the changeless calm of Heaven.

STILL WATERS.

A CRUEL little stream I know,
  Which slowly, slowly crawls between
  The ooze banks, fringed with sedges green,
That serve to bind its feeble flow.

So sheltered that no passing breath
  Of west-wind stirs it; nay, the blast
  Which strips the tall elms and is past,
Scarce wakes to life its face of death.

On its black surface year by year
  The marsh flowers, grown untimely old,
Shed their soft petals like a tear,
  And hopeless drown their faded gold.

Deep in its darkling depths the pike
  Darts with his cruel jaws; by night
The black eels, sinuous, serpent-like,
  Twist like fell ghosts that fear the light.

Spring shuns it, summer loves it not;
  The low fat fields are lit with bloom,
But here the watery sedges rot,
  And all the months are clothed with gloom.

Autumn's first footstep sears to brown
  Its coarse green fringe ; the first cold breath,
Ere yet the oak-leaf flutters down,
  Binds its dull life in icy death.

I hate, I hate you crawling stream!
  Dumb, creeping, murderous wretch, I long
To see the sunlit ripples gleam,
  To hear the torrent's jubilant song.

But you, dull monster, all the years
  Lie rolling on your sullen flood,
And take your fill of mortal tears ;
  Yet, like the Churchmen, spill not blood.

The dark gap in the ice, the boat
  Keel upward, or the drifting oar ;
Or, like of old, the little coat,
  The white clothes heaped upon the shore :

And some young life is over and gone,
  And some fond heart is broken in twain ;
And you flow smoothly, smoothly on,
  Taking no heed for death or pain.

They come and grapple with hooks until
  They reach the slimy deep, where lies
The white thing, very cold and still,
  With death's gaze in its stony eyes.

And you just make a ripple, and then
  Flow smoothly onward : you who slew
Young innocent lives of painted men,
  Long ere the crowded city grew ;

And shall in long years yet to be,
  Pierce unborn mothers with that sharp pain.
Which only a mother feels when he
  Who was her first-born comes again,

A clay-cold heap.   I would that I
  Had but the archangel's flaming brand ;
So would I burn thy dull springs dry,
  And choke thy flow with hills of sand.

Yet why?   Whatever soft souls prate,
  Babbling of universal good,
Love is the sister-child of hate,
  And all good things are bought with blood.

Virtue were not if vice were not,
Nor darkness if there were not light.
Creep on ; fulfil thy murderous lot ;
For wrong has equal life with right.

————o————

IN REGENT STREET.

ONE of the nightly hundreds who pass
Wearily, hopelessly, under the gas.

But the old sad words had a strange new tone,
And the wild laugh seemed to sink to a moan.

So that turning as one constrained to look,
The strange sight stifled the voice of rebuke :

For I looked on a girl's face pure and fair,
Blue-eyed, and crowned with a glory of hair,

Such as my dead child-sister might own,
Were she not a child still, but a woman grown;

Full of the tender graces that come
To the cherished light of an ancient home;

Even to that touch of a high disdain,
Which is born of a name without blot or stain.

Strange; as if one should chance to meet
An angel of light in that sordid street!

" O child, what misery brings you here,
To this place of vileness and weeping and fear?"

" I am no more than the rest," she said,
Proudly averting her beautiful head!

Then no response, till some kinder word
Stole in unawares, and her heart was stirred.

" I was a wife but the other day,
Now I am left without hope or stay!

" Work did I ask?   What work is for you?
What work can those delicate fingers do?

"Service?   But how could I bear to part
From the child with whom I had left my heart?

" Alms ?—Yes, at first ; then a pitiless No :
The State would provide me whither to go.

" But in sordid prisons it laid my head
With the thief and the harlot ; therefore I fled.

" One thing alone had I left untried,
Then I put off the last rag of pride."

" What came ? You were of an honoured race,
Now you must live with your own disgrace."

" But many will buy where few will give,
And I die every day that my child may live."

Motherly love sunk to this !   Ah, well
Teach they not how He went down into hell :

Only blind me in heart and brain,
Or ever I look on the like again.

———o———

FROM THE DESERT.

THOU hast visited me with Thy storms,
And the vials of Thy sore displeasure
Thou hast poured on my head, like a bitter draught
Poured forth without stint or measure ;
Thou hast bruisèd me as flax is bruised ;
Made me clay in the potter's wheel ;
Thou hast hardened Thy face like steel,
And cast down my soul to the ground ;
Burnt my life in the furnace of fire, like dross,
And left me in prison where souls are bound :
Yet my gain is more than my loss.

What if Thou hadst led my soul
To the pastures where dull souls feed ;
And set my steps in smooth paths, far away
From the feet of those that bleed ;
Penned me in low, fat plains,
Where the air is as still as death,
And Thy great winds are sunk to a breath,
And Thy torrents a crawling stream,
And the thick steam of wealth goes up day and night,

Till Thy sun gives a veilèd light,
And heaven shows like a vanished dream !

What if Thou hadst set my feet
With the rich in a gilded room ;
And made me to sit where the scorners sit,
Scoffing at death and doom !
What if I had hardened my heart
With dark counsels line upon line;
And blunted my soul with meat and wine,
Till my ears had grown deaf to the bitter cry
Of the halt and the weak and the impotent ;
Nor hearkened, lapt in a dull content,
To the groanings of those who die!

My being had waxed dull and dead
With the lusts of a gross desire ;
But now Thou hast purged me throughly, and burnt
My shame with a living fire.
So burn me, and purge my will,
Till no vestige of self remain,
And I stand out white without spot or stain.
Then let Thy flaming angel at last

Smite from me all that has been before ;
And sink me, freed from the load of the past,
In Thy dark depths evermore.

———o———

VICTORY.

WE walked together on the sand;
The white cliffs rose and shut out sight ;
And then we rested, hand in hand,
Till evening faded into night.

'Twas the last time,—another day
To busier scenes would see me gone ;
How should I tear my heart away,
And leave her loveless and alone ?

Long time we sat, until the hour
Clanged on our thought, and then I heard
A low, too eloquent sigh of power,
And felt a quiver like a bird.

And marked the lithe form throb and thrill,
As quick the labouring pulses came ;
Great God! how near we are to ill,
Girt by dark gulfs of sin and shame.

" Be glad ! 'tis nature made you so ;
Put off the yoke of childish fears."
" And are there, then, no jails of woe,
No dungeons of despair and tears ? "

And so we rose without a word,
And homeward through the darkness went ;
Dumb, though our inmost hearts were stirred,
And, save in fancy, innocent.

'Tis three years since.   To-day I pressed
The little hand I knew of old :
She bore an infant at her breast,
And on her left the sacred gold.

——o——

CROWNED.

Crowned, royally crowned.
With what crown? With the glow of youth and health,
Long days unclouded, and gilt with wealth;
Rank and honour and luxuries;
A soft life laid in the lap of ease;
Lowly obeisance from all around;
No angry word, or discordant sound
To break on the indolent, slumb'rous air;
Never a sight but that which is fair;
Calm days, sweet and unbroken, ever
Gliding along like a smooth-flowing river?
Is this the crown wherewith he is crowned?

Nay; not this at all.
Then the kingly crown of knowledge and power,
The proud soul on high, in its royal tower,
Glancing down with serene disdain
On the weak souls struggling beneath on the plain;
Fenced by an armour of perfectest steel,
Against all the longings that mortals feel;
Secure in itself, nor deigning a thought

For the fame and the splendour by others sought ?
A passionless calm without pain or strife.
Surely, such is the goal of life.
And is this the crown he is crowned withal ?

Or, with love's diadem,
The fair god naked, yet not afraid ;
Throned in the virgin heart of a maid,
Soul going out to its kindred soul,
With a rush, as when swift streams interfused roll.
A new strange speech, and a radiance bright,
Lighting dark paths with a mystical light ;
Tempering life through the hard-fought years ;
Tempering penury, tempering tears,
Self trodden down, a base weed under feet,
And the white flower of sacrifice springing up sweet,—
Shall he bear on his forehead this marvellous gem ?

Nay ; with none of all these things,
Not for him are these wondrous jewels of price,
Nor the virginal sweetness of sacrifice.
Lonely, unloved, unlearned, obscure,
Only single-eyed always, and pure ;
With no care or thought from his distant youth,

But to gaze afar off on the face of truth.
Content as a patient seeker to scan
The humblest link of the marvellous plan.
Truth's soldier he is, not the less that his name
Shines on no blazoned escutcheon of fame ;
And yet he is crowned, and a king among kings.

——o——

DUMB.

ALL men are poets if they might but tell
The dim ineffable changes which the sight
Of natural beauty works on them : the charm
Of those first days of Spring, when life revives
And all the world is bloom : the white-fringed green
Of summer seas swirling around the base
Of overhanging cliffs ; the golden gleam
Seen from some breezy hill, where far and wide
The fields grow ripe for harvest; or the storm
Smiting the leaden surf, or echoing
On nightly lakes and unsuspected hills,
Revealed in lurid light ; or first perceived,
High in mid heaven, above the rosy clouds,
The everlasting snows.

And Art can move,
To higher minds, an influence as great
As Nature's self; when the rapt gazer marks
The stainless mother folding arms divine
Around the Eternal Child, or pitying Love
Nailed to the dreadful cross, or the white strength
Of happy heathen gods, or serpent coils
Binding the agonized limbs, till from their pain
Is born a thing of beauty for all time.

And more than Nature, more than Art can move
The awakened soul—heroic soaring deeds ;
When the young champion falls in hopeless fight,
Striking for home; or when, by truth constrained.
The martyr goes forth cheerful to his fate—
The dungeon, or the torture, or, more hard,
The averted gaze of friends, the loss of love,
The loneliness of soul, which truth too oft
Gives to reward the faith which casts aside
All things for her; or saintly lives obscure,
Spent in a sweet compassion, till they gain,
Living, some glow of heaven ; or passionate love,
Bathing our poor world in a mystic light,

Seen once, then lost for ever.   These can stir
Life to its depths, till silence grows a load
Too hard to bear, and the rapt soul would fain
Speak with strange tongues which startle as they come,
Like the old saints who spake at Pentecost.

But we are dumb, we are dumb, and may not tell
What stirs within us, though the soul may throb
And tremble with its passion, though the heart
Dissolve in weeping : dumb.   Nature may spread
Sublimest sights of beauty ; Art inspire
High thoughts and pure of God-like sacrifice ;
Yet no word comes.   Heroic daring deeds
Thrill us, yet no word comes ; we are dumb, we are
      dumb,
Save that from finer souls at times may rise,
Once in an age, faint inarticulate sounds,
Low halting tones of wonder, such as come
From children looking on the stars, but still
With power to open to the listening ear
The Fair Divine Unknown, and to unseal
Heaven's inner gates before us evermore.

Ah, few and far between ! The earth grows green,
Fair shows Art's glorious work from year to year,
Great deeds and high are done from day to day,
But the voice comes not which has power to wake
The sleeping soul within, and animate
The beauty which informs them, lending speech
To what before was dumb. They come, they go,
These sweet impressions spent on separate souls,
Like raindrops on the endless ocean-plains,
Lost as they fall. The world rolls on ; lives spring,
Blossom, and fade ; the play of life is played
More vivid than of old, on a wider stage,
With more consummate actors ; yet the dull,
Cold jaws of sullen silence swallow up
The strain, and it is lost. But if we might
Paint all things as they are, find voice to speak
The thoughts now mute within us, let the soul
Trace on its sensitive surface vividly,
As does the sun our features, all the play
Of passion, all the changeful tides of thought,
The mystery, the beauty, the delight,
The fear, the horror, of our lives,—our being

Would blaze up heavenward in a sudden flame,
Spend itself, and be lost.
                                    Wherefore 'tis well
This narrow boundary that hedges in
The strong and weak alike.   Thought could not live,
Nor speech, in that pure æther which girds round
Life's central dwelling-place.   Only the dull
And grosser atmosphere of earth it is
Which vibrates to the sweet birds' song, and brings
Heaven to the wondering ear.   Only the stress,
The pain, the hope, the longing, the constraint
Of limited faculties circling round and round
The grim circumference, and finding naught
Of outlet to the dread unknown beyond,
Can lend the poet voice.   Only the weight,
The dulness of our senses, which makes dumb
And hushes half the finer utterance,
Makes possible the song, and modulates
The too exalted music, that it falls
So soft upon the listening soul, that life,
Not withered by the awful harmony,
Nor drunk with too much sweetness, nor struck blind
By the too vivid presence of the Unknown,

Fulfils its round of duty—elevated,
Not slain by too much splendour—comforted,
Not thunder-smitten—soothed, not laid asleep—
And ever, through the devious maze of being,
Fares in slow narrowing cycles to the end.

——o——

FAITH WITHOUT SIGHT.

No angel comes to us to tell
　　Glad news of our belovèd dead ;
Nor at the old familiar board,
　　They sit among us, breaking bread.

Three days we wait before the tomb,
　　Nay, life-long years ; and yet no more,
For all our passionate tears, we find
　　The stone rolled backward from the door.

Yet are they risen as He is risen ;
　　For no eternal loss we grieve.
Blessèd are they who ask no sign,
　　And, never having seen, believe.

——o——

CAGED.

ALAS for fame ! I saw a genius sit,
 Draining full bumpers with a trembling hand,
And roll out rhapsodies of folly, lit
 By soaring fancies hard to understand.
Lonely he seemed, whom all men should admire ;
 And some were there who sneered a covert sneer,
Quenching with logic cold the sacred fire ;
 And one who hardly checked a rising tear,

Because life's order binds with chains of steel
 The struggling individual soul ; because
The fair fine flower of life doth oft conceal
 A hidden worm which always frets and gnaws
The inner heart from which its perfumes come,
 And round the deep-set core of golden fire
Foul creeping creatures make their constant home—
 Black hatred, wild revolt, and gross desire.

What is this bar that Nature loves to place
 Before the too aspiring heart and brain,—
Bringing down goodly hopes to deep disgrace,
 Keeping high pleasure balanced by low pain,

Pure thoughts by secret failings, subtler joys
   With grosser sense or hopeless depths of woe,—
Setting our lives in barren counterpoise,
   Which says, Thus far, no further shalt thou go.

Is it that Nature, envious of her own,
   Even as the fabled gods of primal years,
Because to too great stature it is grown,
   Hates her consummate work, and inly fears
Lest the soul, once enfranchised, soar too high,
   Up to some Spiritual place of Souls,
Where the world's feeble echoes faint and die,
   And in fine waves a purer æther rolls?

There is no infinite in Nature.   All
   Is finite, set within a self-made bound.
Thought builds round space itself a brazen wall,
   And hates the barren cycle's endless round.
Life grown too perfect is not life at all;
   Some hidden discords sweeten every strain;
No virtue is, where is no power to fall,
   Nor true delight without a touch of pain.

And this it is that limits evermore
 The life of man to this its low estate,
And gives the soul's light pinions power to soar
 Only a little space toward heaven's gate.
Creatures we are of the earth, and not the sky,
 Bound down, constrained, confined; and yet 'tis
 well :
No angel's wings are ours to mount on high,
 No chains have power to keep our souls in hell.

And since to realms of thought we may aspire,
 Higher than these in which we breathe and are,
And know within the same creative fire
 As that which lights and warms the furthest star,
So should our restless spirits grow content
 With what is theirs, nor covet to be free ;
Since boundless power is oft most impotent,
 And narrow bonds the truest liberty.

——o——

TOO MUCH KNOWLEDGE.

Oh, if we had but eyes to see
    The glory which around us lies,
To read the secrets of the earth,
    And know the splendours of the skies ;

And if we had but ears to hear
    The psalm of life which upward rolls
From desert tent and city street,
    From every meeting-place of souls ;

And if we had but tongues to tell
    The dumb thoughts that shall ne'er be heard,
The inarticulate prayers which rise
    From hearts by passionate yearnings stirred,—

Our souls would parch, like Semele's,
    When her dread Lord blazed forth confessed.
Ah, sometimes too much knowledge blights,
    And ignorance indeed is blest !

—— o ——

ON A FLIGHT OF LADY-BIRDS.

OVER the summer sea,
  Floating on delicate wings,
Comes an unnumbered host
  Of beautiful fragile things;
Whence they have come, or what
  Blind impulse has forced them here,
What still voice marshalled them out
  Over wide seas without fear,
You cannot tell, nor I.

But to-day the air is thick
  With these strangers from far away :
On hot piers and drifting ships
  The weary travellers stay.
On the sands where to-night they will drown,
  On the busy waterside street,
Trampled in myriads down
  By the careless wayfarers' feet,
The beautiful creatures lie.

Who knows what myriads have sunk
  To drown in the oily waves,
Till all our sea-side world shows
  Like a grave-yard crowded with graves?
Humble creatures and small,
  How shall the Will which sways
This enormous unresting ball,
  Through endless cycles of days,
Take thought for them or care?

And yet, if the greatest of kings,
  With the wisest of sages combined,
Never could both devise—
  Strong arm and inventive mind—
So wondrous a shining coat,
  Such delicate wings and free,
As have these small creatures who float
  Over the breathless sea
On this summer morning so fair;

  *   *   *   *   *

And the life, the wonderful life,
  Which not all the wisdom of earth
Can give to the humblest creature that moves—

The mystical process of birth—
The nameless principle which doth lurk
   Far away beyond atom, or monad, or cell,
And is truly His own most marvellous work-
   Was it good to give it, or, given, well
To squander it thus away?

For surely a man might think
   So precious a gift and grand—
God's essence in part—should be meted out
   With a thrifty and grudging hand.
And hard by, on the yellowing corn,
   Myriads of tiny jaws
Are bringing the husbandman's labour to scorn,
   And the cankerworm frets and gnaws,
Which was made for these for a prey.

For a prey for these? but, oh!
   Who shall read us the riddle of life—
The prodigal waste, which nought can redress
   But a cycle of sorrow and strife,
The continual sequence of pain,
   The perpetual triumph of wrong,

The whole creation in travail to make
A victory for the strong,
And not with frail insects alone?

For is not the scheme worked out
Among us who are raised so high?
Are there no wasted minds among men—
No hearts that aspire and sigh
For the hopes which the years steal away,
For the labour they love, and its meed of fame,
And feel the bright blade grow rusted within,
Or are born to inherited shame,
And a portion with those that groan?

How are we fettered and caged
Within our dark prison-house here!
We are made to look for a loving plan;
We find everywhere sorrow and fear.
We look for the triumph of Good;
And, from all the wide world around,
The lives that are spent cry upward to heaven,
From the slaughter-house of the ground,
Till we feel that Evil is lord.

And yet are we bound to believe,
    Because all our nature is so,
In a Ruler touched by an infinite ruth
    For all His creatures below.
Bound, though a mocking fiend point,
    To the waste, and ruin, and pain—
Bound, though our souls should be bowed in despair—
    Bound, though wrong triumph again and again,
And we cannot answer a word.

——o ——

ON AN OLD MINSTER.

OLD minster, when my years were few,
    And life seemed endless to the boy ;
    Still calm and vivid is the joy
With which I gazed and thought on you.

Thin shaft and flower-wrought capital,
    High-springing arch, and blazoned pane,
    Quaint gurgoyles stretching heads profane,
And stately throne and carven stall.

The long nave lost in vaporous gray,
    The mailed recumbent forms which wait,
    In mockery of earthly state,
The coming of the dreadful day.

The haunted aisles, the gathering gloom,
    By some stray shaft of eve made fair :
    The stillness of the mouldering air,
The faded legends of the tomb.

I loved them all.   What care had I,—
    I, the young heir of all the past,—
    That neither youth nor life might last,
That all things living came to die !

The past was spent, the past was done,
    The present was my own to hold ;
    Far off within a haze of gold
Stretched the fair future, scarce begun.

For me did pious builders rear
    Those reverend walls ; for me the song
    Of supplication, ages long,
Had gone up daily, year by year.

On an Old Minster.

And thus I loved you ; but to-day
   The long past near and nearer shows ;
   Less bright, more clear, the future grows,
And all the world is growing gray.

But you scarce bear a deeper trace
   Of time upon your solemn brow ;
   No sadder, stiller, grayer now,
Than when I loved your reverend face.

And you shall be when I am not ;
   And you shall be a thing of joy
   To many a frank and careless boy
When I and mine are long forgot.

Grave priests shall here with holy rage,
   Whose grandsires are as yet unborn,
   Lash, with fierce words of saintly scorn,
The heats of youth, the greed of age.

Proud prelates sit on that high throne,
   Whose young forefathers drive the plough :
   While Norman lineage nods below,
In aged tramp or withered crone.

And white-haired traders feign to pray,
    Sunk deep in thoughts of gain and gold ;
    And sweet flower-faces growing old,
Give place to fresher blooms than they.

With such new shape of creed and rite
    As none now living may foretell ;
    A faith of love which needs not hell,
A stainless worship, pure and white.

Or, may be, some reverting change
    To the old faith of vanished days :
    The incensed air, the mystic praise,
The barbarous ritual, quaint and strange.

Who knows ?   But they are wrong who say
    Man's work is brief and quickly past ;
    If you through all these centuries last,
While they who built you pass away.

The wind, the rain, the sand, are slow ;
    Man fades before his work ; scant trace
    Time's finger findeth to efface
Of him whom seventy years lay low.

The grass grows green awhile, and then
 Is as before ; the work he made
 Casts on his grave a reverend shade
Through long successive lives of men.

But he ! where is he ? Lo, his name
 Has vanished from his wonted place,
 Unknown his tongue, his creed, his race ;
Unknown his soaring hopes of fame.

Only the creatures of the brain,—
 Just laws, wise precepts, deathless verse ;
 These weave a chaplet for the hearse,
And through all change unchanged remain.

These will I love as age creeps on ;
 Gray minster, these are ever young ;
 These shall be read and loved and sung
When every stone of you is gone.

No hands have built the monument
 Which to all ages shall endure ;—
 High thoughts and fancies, sweet and pure,
Lives in the quest of goodness spent.

These, though no visible forms confine
  Their spiritual essence fair ;
Are deathless as the soul they bear,
  And, as its Maker is, divine.

———o———

THE BITTER HARVEST.

WHO reaps the harvest of his soul,
  And garners up thought's golden grain,
For him in vain life's tempests rave,
  Fate's rude shocks buffet him in vain.

The storms which shipwreck feebler souls,
  Beat harmlessly on him ; the wind,
Which whirls away the domes of pride,
  Braces the sinews of his mind.

He is set within a tower of strength,
  Beyond thick walls and cloisters still ;
Where, as he sits, no faintest breath
  Stirs the smooth current of his will.

He is stretched in a smiling valley where,
  When hills are dark, the full sun shines ;
Brings gold upon the waving fields,
  And purple clusters on the vines.

He lies in a boundless sylvan shade,
  While all the fields are parched around ,
And hears a sweet bird, singing, singing,
  With one clear monotone of sound.

Far, far away from the busy crowd
  And chaffering of the mart, he stands,
Like a statue on a lonely hill,
  Pondering a scroll within its hands.

Or one who, from high convent walls,
  Looks down at eve upon the plain,
And sees the children at their sport,
  And turns to chant and prayer again.

So rich, and yet so very poor,
  So fruitful, yet so void of fruit ;
Removed from human hopes and fears,
  Far as the man is from the brute.

So troubled, 'neath a face of calm ;
   So bound with chains, though seeming free ;
So dead, though with a name to live,
   That it were better not to be.

———o———

OF LOVE AND SLEEP.

I SAW Sleep stand by an enchanted wood,
   Thick lashes drooping o'er her heavy eyes ;
Leaning against a flower-cupped tree she stood,
   The night air gently breathed with slumbrous sighs.
Such cloak of silence o'er the world was spread,
As on Nile sands clings round the mighty dead.

About her birds were dumb, and blooms were bowed,
   And a thick heavy sweetness filled the air ;
White robed she seemed, and hidden as in a cloud,
   A star-like jewel in her raven hair.
Downward to earth her cold torch would she turn
With feeble fires that might no longer burn.

And in her languid limbs and loosened zone
  Such beauty dwelt ; and in her rippling hair,
As of old time was hers, and hers alone,
  The mother of gods and men divinely fair :
When whiter than white foam or sand she lay,
The fairest thing beneath the eye of day.

To her came Love, a comely youth and strong,
  Fair as the morning of a day in June ;
Around him breathed a faint sweet air of song,
  And his limbs moved as to a joyous tune :
With golden locks blown back, and eyes aflame,
To where the sleeping maiden leant, he came.

Then they twain passed within that mystic grove
  Together, and with them I, myself unseen.
Oh, strange, sweet land ! wherein all men may prove
  The things they would, the things which might have
    been ;
Hopeless hopes blossom, withered youth revives,
And sunshine comes again to darkened lives.

What sights were theirs in that blest wonder-land ?
  See, the white mountain-summits, framed in cloud.

Redden with sunset ; while below them stand
   The solemn pine-woods like a funeral crowd ;
And lower still the vineyards twine, and make
A double vintage in the tranquil lake.

Or, after storm-tost nights, by some sea isle
   The sudden tropical morning breaks ; and lo !
Bright birds and feathery palms, the green hills smile,
   Strange barks, with swarthy crews, dart to and fro ;
And on the blue bay, glittering like a crown,
The white domes of some fair historic town.

Or, they fare northward, ever northward still,
   At midnight, under the unsetting sun ;
O'er endless snows, from hill to icy hill,
   Where silence reigns with death, and life is done :
Till from the North a sweet wind suddenly ;
And hark ! the warm waves of the fabulous sea.

Or, some still eve, when summer days are long,
   And the mown hay is sweet, and wheat is green,
They hear some wood-bird sing the old fair song
   Of joys to be, greater than yet have been.

Stretched 'neath the snowy hawthorn, till the star,
Hung high in heaven, warns them that home is far.

Or, on the herbless, sun-struck hills, by night,
   Under the silent peaks, they hear the loud
Wild flutes; and onward, by the ghostly light,
   Whirled in nude dances, sweeps the maddened crowd;
Till the fierce eddy seize them, and they prove
The shame, the rapture, of unfettered love.

Or, by the sacred hearth they seem to sit,
   While firelight gleams on many a sunny head;
At that fair hour, before the lamp is lit,
   When hearts are fullest, though no word be said. –
When the world fades, and rank and wealth and fame,
Seem, matched with this, no better than a name.

All these they knew; and then a breeze of day
   Stirred the dark wood; and then they seemed to come
Forth with reluctant feet among the gray,
   Bare fields, unfanciful; and all the flame
Was burnt from out Love's eyes, and from his hair,
And his smooth cheek was marked with lines of care.

And paler showed the maid, more pure and white
And holier than before.   But when I said,
"Sweet eyes, be opened;" lo, the unveilèd sight
Was as the awful vision of the dead !
Then knew I, breathing slow, with difficult breath,
That Love was one with Life, and Sleep with Death.

------o------

BLIND.

THE girl who from her father's door
    Sees the cold storm-cloud sweep the sea,
Cries, wrestling with her anguish sore,
    My love ! my love ! ah, where is he ?
And locks her fear within her breast,
    Sickening ; while 'neath the breathless blaze
He lies, and dreams, in broken rest,
    Of homely faces,—happier days.

But when a calm is on the deep,
    And scarcely from the quivering blue,
The waves, soft murmur, half asleep,
    Speaks hope that he is well, and true:

The brave ship sinks to rise no more
    Beneath the thunderous surge; and he,
A pale corpse floating on the sea,
    Or dashed like seaweed on the shore.

—— o ——

TO HER PICTURE.

As one who on a lonely bed of pain
    Feels the soft hand he felt when he was young;
Or, who at eve, on some far Eastern plain,
    Hears the old songs once by his mother sung:
So to me, looking on thy portrait, dear,
Thou and my youth and love are ever near.

It may be that the painter failed to show,
    How should he not? the soul within thine eyes,—
Their blue unruffled depths, thy cheeks aglow
    With virgin blushes that unbidden rise;
Thy coral lips, thy white neck, round, and fair,
Or the sweet prodigal auburn of thy hair.

How should he? Not for him thou wast, but me;
    Love shot no sudden splendour in his eyes;

Love guided not his hand, content to see
  Mere beauty, as of sunset-hills or skies ;
Nor soothed his dull ear with the mystic strain,
Heard once a life, and nevermore again.

Only the lovely shell he saw ; the cloak,
  The perfect vesture of the hidden soul.
Not for his eyes thy slumbering angel woke,
  Stretched in deep sleep, where love's broad waters roll
Had he but seen her wings of silver move,
He had forgot to paint, and learned to love.

Yet is his skill to me for ever blest,
  For that which it has left of grace and truth ;
Those sweet eyes shine, yet need no time of rest,
  Still thy fair cheek retains its rounded youth.
In wakeful nights I light my lamp, and know
The same dear face I knew long years ago.

Yet worn am I, too old for love, and gray.
  Too faithful heart, thou shouldst not still abide
With such as I, nor longer deign to stay :
  These are the follies wiser worldlings chide.

Thou wouldst transfer those glances, wert thou wise,
To younger lives and more responsive eyes.

Ah ! no, remain ; not thus you looked of yore ;
   Another, perhaps more worthy, bore the prize ;
I could not tell you then the love I bore,
   Or read the soft requital in your eyes ;
Now no change comes, now thou art always kind,
Then thou wast cold and changeful as the wind.

—o—

THE RETURN.

He stood above the well-known shore ;
   Behind, the sea stretched dull and gray ;
And slowly with the breeze of morn
   The great ship forged away.

Almost he wished she might return,
   And speed him to some further change ;
The old scenes greeted him again,
   And yet all things were strange.

There were the dreams he used to dream
    In the long nights when day was here;
The shady Sunday path to church,
    The winding brooklet clear.

The woods where violets grew in Spring,
    The fallow where they chased the hare,
The gable peeping through the elms,
    All filled him with despair.

For all was there except the past—
    The past, his youth for dross had sold!
The past which after-years in vain
    Prize more than all their gold.

Then age fell on him with a flash,
    Time smote him, and his soul grew gray;
And thoughts in busier scenes unknown,
    Chased youth and hope away.

The past, which seemed so near before,
    A step might gain it, came to be
A low cloud sunk beyond a gulf,
    Wider than any sea.

Nor what the present had in store,
  Knowing; at last his great suspense
Grew to a bitter load of pain,
  Too great for mortal sense.

So, by the well-known paths at last,
  He gained the well remembered door,
Sick for a voice which he should hear,
  Ah ! never, never, more.

Strange children round, a stranger's face
  Of wonder, so the dream was o'er.
He turned ; the dead past comes not back,
  No, never, never, more.

———o———

FOR EVER.

FOR ever and for ever
  The changeless oceans roar ;
And dash their thundering surges down
  Upon the sounding shore :
Yet this swift soul, this lightning will,
Shall these, while they roll on, be still?

For ever and for ever
    The eternal mountains rise,
And lift their virgin snows on high
    To meet the silent skies.
Yet shall this soul which measures all,
While these stand steadfast, sink and fall?

For ever and for ever
    The swift suns roll through space;
From age to age they wax and wane,
    Each in its ordered place:
Yet shall the soul, whose inner eye
Foretells their cycles, fade and die.

For ever and for ever
    We have been, and we are,
Unchanging as the ocean wave,
    Unresting as the star:
Though suns stand still, and time be o'er,
We are, and shall be, evermore.

BEHIND THE VEIL.

I PACED along
The dim cathedral wrapped in reverend gloom ;
I heard the sweet child's song
Spring upwards like a fountain ; and the boom
Of the tempestuous organ-music swell ;
The hushed low voices, and the silvery bell ;
The incense-laden air; the kneeling throng:
I knew them all, and seemed to hear the cry
Of countless myriads, rising deep and strong,—
Help us ! we faint, we die.
Our knees are weak, our eyes are blind;
We seek what we shall never find.
Show but Thy face, and we are Thine,
Unknown, Ineffable, Divine!

I heard the loud
Muezzin from the slender minaret call
To prayer, to prayer ; and lo! the busy crowd,
Merchant and prince and water-carrier, all
Turned from the world, and, rapt in worship, knelt,
Facing the holy city ; and I felt

O

That from those myriads kneeling, prostrate, bowed,
A low moan rises to the throne on high,—
Not shut out quite by error's thickest cloud,—
Help us ! we faint, we die.
Our knees are weak, our eyes are blind;
We seek what we shall never find.
Show but Thy face, and we are Thine,
Unknown, Ineffable, Divine.

                              I stood before
The glaring temples on the burning plains ;
I heard the hideous roar
Rise to the stars to drown the shrieks of pain,
What time the murderous idol swept along.
I listened to the innocent, mystic song,
Breathed to the jewelled Lotus evermore,
In the elder lands, through the ages, like a sigh,
And heard in low, sweet chant, and hateful roar,—
Help us ! we faint, we die.
Our knees are weak, our eyes are blind;
We seek what we shall never find.
Show but Thy face, and we are Thine,
Unknown, Ineffable, Divine !

Ay; everywhere
Echoes the same exceeding bitter cry.
Yet can the Father bear
To hide His presence from the children's eye;
Lets loose on good and bad the plague and sword;
And though wrong triumph, answers not a word?
Only deep down in the heart doth He declare
His constant presence; there, though the outward sky
Be darkened, shines a little speck of fair,—
A light which cannot die.
Though knees be weak, and eyes be blind;
Though we may seek, and never find;
Here doth His hidden glory shine,
Unknown, Ineffable, Divine.

———o———

TO AN OLD FRIEND.

THERE is a friend I would not lose,
   His home is the old church tower;
Summer and winter, day and night,
   He preaches the knell of the hour.

On sweet June nights, when the birds and the flowers
  Are asleep, and the world is still ;
And only the burning nightingales peal
  From the hawthorns under the hill.

Or in winter cold, when the wild winds rave,
  Or the frozen world lies dead ;
And his voice sounds clear when the red bolt falls,
  And the thunder peal rolls overhead.

In the clear summer morn, when the sun has just risen,
  Says my old friend, half mournfully, " Five ;"
And rest is done for the honest hands
  Whose lot is to labour and strive.

And when the shadows begin to slope,
  And the day's long trouble is o'er ;
He gladly says, "Six," and the silent fields
  Sound with echoes of labour no more.

On Sunday mornings, when chimes are done,
  My old friend says gravely, " Eleven ;"
And the morning hymn rises from childish lips,
  With a sound like the sounds of heaven.

He raises his voice, and the schoolroom fills
  With bright faces, day after day ;
He has only to whisper, and out in a trice
  Bursts a volley of mad-caps at play.

And summer and winter, for young and old,
  That grave voice will sound in our ears;
Till our souls have passed over the silent stream
  Far away from this valley of tears.

----o----

VISIONS.

Oft in the blazing summer noon,
And oft beneath the frosty moon,
When earth and air were hushed and still,
And absolute silence seemed to fill
The farthest border-lands of space,
I loved in childish thought to trace
Glimpses of change, which might transform
The voiceless calm to furious storm ;
Broke the dull spell, which comes to bind
In after years the sluggish mind;

And pictured, borne on fancy's wings,
The end of all created things.

Then have I seen with dreaming eye,
The blue depths of the vaulted sky
Rent without noise ; and in their stead
A wonder-world of fancy spread,
A golden city, with domes and spires,
Lit by a strange sun's mystic fires.
Portals of dazzling chrysolite,
Long colonnades of purest white ;
Streets paved with gold and jewels rare ;
And higher, in the ambient air,
A shining Presence undefined :
Swift seraphs stooping swift as wind
From pole to pole, and that vast throng
Which peopled Dante's world of song ;
The last great inquest, which shall close
The tale of human joys and woes ;
The dreadful Judge, the opening tomb,
And all the mystery of doom.
Then woke to find the vision vain,
And sun or moon shine calm again.

No longer, save in memory's glass,
These vanished visions come and pass ;
The clearer light of fuller day
Has chased these earlier dreams away.
Faith's eye grows dim with too much light,
And fancy flies our clearer sight.
But shall we mourn her day is o'er,
That these rapt visions come no more ?
Nay ; knowledge has its splendours too,
Brighter than Fancy's brightest hue.
I gaze now on the heavens, and see
How, midst their vast immensity,
By cosmic laws the planets roll,
Sped onwards by a central soul;
How farther still, and still more far,
World beyond world, star beyond star,
So many, and so far, that speech
And thought must fail the sum to reach.
This universe of nature teems
With things more strange than fancy's dreams ;
And so at length, with clearer eye,
Soar beyond childhood's painted sky,
Up to the Lord of great and small,

Not onewhere, but pervading all :
Who made the music of the spheres,
And yet inclines an ear that hears
The faintest prayer, the humblest sigh,
The strong man's groan, the childish cry :
Who guides the stars, yet without whom
No humblest floweret comes to bloom,
No lowliest creature comes to birth,
No dead leaf flutters to the earth :
Who breathed into our souls the breath,
Which neither time nor change nor death,
Nor hurtling suns at random hurled
And dashed together, world on world,
Can ever kill or quench, till He
Bends down, and bids them not to be.

———o———

BABYLON.

THIS is Great Babylon that is builded ;
    Mark well her domes and towers of pride,
    The throng in her long streets fair and wide,
Her gleaming palaces gilded.

Mark her well for what she is now.
  A little time since, where she stands to-day,
  No foot-step stirred on the desolate gray,
Nor keel on her dull river's flow.

A place of foulness and shame and sorrow,
  Where men sit at feasts while their brethren perish ;
  Where young lives, left lonely with none to cherish,
Grow ripe for a shameful morrow ;

Of lofty aims and saintly endeavour,
  Of pure souls waging continual strife,
  Fierce as the conflict of death with life,
With the wrong that is done for ever;

Of careless lives lost in pursuit of pleasure,
  Wasted, yet missing the end which they sought ;
  Of calm days yielded to patient thought,
Adding something to man's great treasure.

Mark her well, for the mystery-play
  Will be played out ere long, as others before ;
  And then the dead river will steal on once more
Through sad plains silent and gray.

DOUBT.

Who but has seen
Once in his life, when youth and health ran high,
The fair, clear face of truth
        Grow dark to his eye?
        Who but has known
Cold mists of doubt and icy questionings
Creep round him like a nightmare, blotting out
        The sight of better things.

        A hopeless hour,
When all the voices of the soul are dumb,
When o'er the tossing seas
        No light may come,
        When God and right
Are gone, and seated on the empty throne
Are dull philosophies and words of wind,
        Making His praise their own.

        Better than this,
The burning sins of youth, the greed of age,
Than thus to live inane;
        To sit and read,

Doubt.

And with blind brain
Daily to treasure up a deadly doubt,
And live a life from which the light has fled,
And faith's pure fire gone out.

Until at last,
For some blest souls, but never here for all,
Burns out a sudden light,
And breaks the thrall,
And doubt has fled,
And the soul rises, with a clearer sight
For this its pain, its sorrow, its despair,
To God and truth and right.

Plead we for those
Gently and humbly, as befitteth men
On whom the same chill shade
Broods now as then.
So shall they learn
How an eternal wisdom rules above,
And all the cords of Being are gathered u p
In an unfailing love.

—o—

ST. DAVID'S HEAD.

SALT sprays deluge it, wild waves buffet it, hurricanes
    rave;
Summer and winter, the depths of the ocean girdle it
    round;
In leaden dawns, in golden noon-tides, in silvery moon-
    light
Never it ceases to hear the old sea's mystical sound.
      Surges vex it evermore
      By gray cave and sounding shore.

Think of the numberless far-away centuries, long before
    man,
When the hot earth with monsters teemed, and with
    monsters the deep,
And the red sun loomed faint, and the moon was caught
    fast in the motionless air,
And the warm waves seethed through the haze in a secular
    sleep.
      Rock was here and headland then,
      Ere the little lives of men.

Over it long the mastodons crashed through the tropical
  forest,
And the great bats swooped overhead through the half-
  defined blue ;
Then they passed, and the hideous ape-man, speechless
  and half-erect,
Through weary ages of time tore and gibbered and slew.
    Grayer skies and chiller air,
    But the self-same rock was there.

Then the savage came and went, and Briton and Roman
  and Saxon,
Till our England grew rich and great, and her white
  sails covered the sea ;
Thus through all this long story of ours, civil progress
  and vanquished foeman,
From Crecy to Trafalgar, from the bondsman down to
  the free,
    Still those dark rocks, and beneath
    Keeps the sea its face of death.

So it shall be when the tide of our greatness has ebbed
  to the shallows ;

So when there floats not a ship on this storm-tossed
westerly main,
Hard by, the minster crumbles, the city has shrunk to a
village ;
Thus shall we shrink one day, and our forests be path-
less again ;
And the headland stern shall stand,
Guarding an undiscovered land.

Vex it, O changeless ocean ; rave round it, tempests
unceasing ;
Sink it, great earthquakes, deep in the depths of the
fathomless sea ;
Burn them, fierce fires of the centre, burn rock and
ocean together,
Till the red globe flare throughout space, through the
ages to be.
Cease, make an end, dull world, begone ;
How shall I cease while you roll on ?

Time, oh, horrible !   Space, oh, terrible ! infinite void :
Dreadful abysses of being ! blighting a finite brain ;
How shall the creatures of thought subsist, when the
thinker ceases ?

Begone, dull figments, be done ! not alone shall you dare
 to remain.
  Without me you yourselves must fall ;
  I hold the measure of you all.

—— o ——

IN VOLHYNIA.

In Volhynia the peasant mothers,
 When spring-time brings back the leaves,
And the first swallows dart and twitter
 Under the cottage eaves,—

Sit mute at their windows, and listen,
 With eyes brimming over with tears,
To the broken sounds which are wafted
 To their eager watching ears.

And throw out bread and honey
 To the birds as they scintillate by ;
And hearts full of yearning and longing,
 Borne out on the wings of a sigh.

For they think that their dear lost children,
   The little ones who are gone,
Come back thus to the heartsick mothers
   Who are toiling and sorrowing on.

And those sun-lit wings and flashing
   White breasts, to their tear-dimmed eyes
Bring visions of white child-angels
   Floating in Paradise.

And again to the sounds they hearken,
   Which grew silent while incomplete,
The music of childish laughter,
   The patter of baby feet.

Till the hearts which are barren and childless,
   The homes which are empty and cold :
The nests whence the young have departed,
   Are filled with young life as of old.

Thus each spring, to those peasant mothers,
   Comes the old past again and again ;
And those sad hearts quicken and blossom,
   In a rapture of sorrowless pain.

THE LIVING PAST.

O FAITHFUL souls that watch and yearn,
    Expectant of the coming light,
With kindling hearts and eyes that burn
    With hope to see the rule of right;

The time of peace and of good will,
    When the thick clouds of wrong and pain
Roll up as from a shining hill,
    And never more descend again;

The perfect day, the golden year,
    The end of sorrow and of sighs;
Whether the heavenly change be here,
    Or far beyond the sunset skies,—

I cherish you, I love your faith,
    I long with you 'that this may be;
But hark, a dreary voice which saith,
    " Vain dreamer, what were it to thee!"

For though the blest hour strike before
    Another sunrise vex the earth,
And pain and evil rule no more,
    But vanish in the newer birth,—

Though war and hatred come to cease,
    And sorrow be no more, nor sin,
And in their stead an endless peace
    Its fair unbroken reign begin,—

What comfort have ye?   What shall blot
    The memories of bitter years,
Of joys which have been, but are not,
    And floods of unforgotten tears?

The painful records graven clear
    On carven rock or deathless page;
The long unceasing reign of fear,
    The weary tale of lust and rage;

The ills whose dark sum baffles thought,
    Done day by day beneath the sun?
"That which is done," the old sage taught,
    " Not God Himself can make undone."

For that which has been still must live,
  And 'neath the shallow Present last.
Oh, who will sweet oblivion give,
  Who free us from the dreadful Past!

———o———

CHANGES.

You see that tall house opposite?
  Three times within the fleeting year,
  Since last the summer-time was here,
Great changes have gone over it.

For first a bridal bright and gay
  Filled the long street with riotous sound;
  And amid smiles from all around,
The newly-wedded passed away.

And when the violets came once more,
  And lambs were born, a concourse went,
  Still gayer, still more innocent,
To christening from that stately door.

And now the mute house dull and drear,
   From blinded eyes, stares blank and white ;
   And amid dust and glaring light,
The black lines slowly disappear.

——o——

PERIKLES.

IT was a sick man's chamber, and therein,
In broken slumber, breathing out his life,
The noblest son of Hellas, Perikles.
He had seen the people falling thick around him,
Plague-stricken, yet unmurmuring, till at last
Grief conquered better nature, and they cursed
Him whose smooth tongue had lured them step by step
To pestilence and famine.   He had seen
His youngest born and dearest Paralus
Fall like a flower untimely ; yet he stood
Unmoved through all, and locked within his breast
His sorrow and his anger ; for he saw
Bright sunbeams glance athwart the cloud of ill,
And joy for Hellas, even as earth and sea
Smile sweeter for the beating of the storm.

So he had made his prayer unto the gods,
If haply he might see with his own eyes
The glorious Athens which his soul foreknew.
But either fate is more than Zeus himself,
Or the gods take no heed for mortal men;
For now, ere he was old, his time was come
To die, while yet the clouds were dark and lowering,
Before one ray of hope had beamed upon him.
Athenè, to die thus was hard indeed!

Yet he lay very quiet, ebbing out
Day after day, well knowing that the end
Came nearer daily not without a hope;
That he who loved his country more than life,
And honour more than her, might seem at last
Worthy to tread Olympus, and to see
The shining faces of the eternal gods.

And one day, when the fountains of his life
Ran small and low, came many sorrowing friends
With kindly lies of comfort: some to bring
News of successful battle; how the State
Was rising from despair; or how the plague

Was waning from among them, knowing well
That this to him was more than life itself,
The welfare of his Athens ; some to breathe
Kind words of pious prayer, that the great gods
Might spare him to their city, which had else
Champion nor saviour.   Not a word he spake,
But pointed smiling to the amulets
Which woman's blinder faith had hung around him :
An eloquent smile, for what it said was this,—
" Think ye that I who have lived all my life
Striving to see Truth's face, I who have sat
Beneath the planes, and heard the sages tell
Of Life and Death, and God's unerring will,
But that the end were near, would suffer this ?"

And then he closed his eyes as if to sleep,
And each man knew within his inner soul
That death was hard upon him.   As they gazed
On that tall wasted form stretched out before them,
They seemed to look on Athens.   So their souls
Were kindled, and they spake in glowing words
Of all his glorious deeds by land and sea,
And so bethought them of the eloquent tongue

Which there was mute among them ; how his honour
Spurned at the bribe which won Themistokles ;
And how since they were young who now grew old,
He held the reins of state so wise and pure,
He showed like Zeus among his fellow-men ;
And, firing with the theme, discoursed with pride
Of Athens' greatness, mistress of the seas ;
"And who had built her up but Perikles!"
"And who could save her then but Perikles!"
"And who was truer soul than Perikles!"

Till, when a silence held them, not because
They had no other glorious deeds to tell,
But that their hearts were strung too high for words,
Again once more the sweet calm voice, " Oh, friends,
When you lie helpless as I lie to-day,
The chiefest solace of your end will be,
Not in the memory of battles won,
Or widened empire, or the fame of men.
For what are men but ministers of Zeus !
Defeat or victory, disgrace or fame,
Lie 'tween his knees to measure as he will.
Be this your glory rather, as 'tis mine,—

Never in life's long fight to have done a wrong
To the humblest son of Athens!"
                                        So he spake
Words dying not unworthy of his life.

———o———

ALONE.

WHAT shall it profit a man
To have stood by the source of things,
To have spent the fair years of his youthful prime
In mystical questionings ;
To have scaled the lovely height,
While his brothers slept below ;
To have seen the vision bright
Which but few on earth may know,—
If when his task be done
He lives his life alone?
If in the busy street
None come whom he may greet?
If in his lonely room
With the night the shadows deepen into ghostly
    shapes of gloom?

It may be his soul may say,
"I have gained me a splendid dower;
I can look around on the toiling crowd,
With the pride of a conscious power.
I can hear the passer-by
Tell of all my world-wide fame;
I have friends I shall not see
Who dwell fondly on my name.
If the sweet smile of wife
Light not my joyless life,
If to my silent home
No childish laughter come,
Shall I no solace find
In communion with the monarchs of the fair broad
    realm of mind?"

But when sickness wears him, or age
Creeps on, and his soul doth yearn
For the tender hand and the soothing voice
That shall nevermore return;
When the crowd of careless friends,
Not unkind, but each one set
Safe within white walls of home,

All the world without forget,—
Shall not old memories rise
'Twixt book and weary eyes,
Till knowledge come to seem
A profitless vague dream?
Shall not he sometimes sigh
For the careless past unlearnèd, and the happy
   days gone by?

Ah! not to be happy alone,
Are men sent, or to be glad.
Oft-times the sweetest music is made
By the voices of the sad.
The thinker oft is bent
By a too-great load of thought;
The discoverer's soul grows sick
With the secret vainly sought;
Lonely may be the home,
No breath of fame may come,
Yet through their lives doth shine
A purple light Divine,
And a nobler pain they prove
Than the bloom of lower pleasures, or the fleeting
   spell of love.

SEA VOICES.

PEACE, moaning Sea ; what tale have you to tell ?
What mystic tidings, all unknown before ?
Whether you break in thunder on the shore,
Or whisper like the voice within the shell,
O moaning Sea, I know your burden well.

'Tis but the old dull tale, filled full of pain ;
   The finger on the dial-plate of time,
   Advancing slow with pitiless beat sublime,
As stoops the day upon the fading plain ;
And that has been which may not be again.

The voice of yearning, deep but scarce expressed,
   For something which is not, but may be yet ;
   Too full of sad continuance to forget,
Too troubled with desires to be at rest,
Too self-conflicting ever to be blest.

The voice of hopes and aspirations high,
   Swallowed in sand, or shivered on the rock ;
   Tumultuous life dashed down with sudden shock ;

And passionate protests, narrowed to a sigh,
From hearts too weak to live,—too strong to die.

The voice of old beliefs which long have fled,
    Gone with a shriek, and leaving naught behind,
    But some vague utterance, cold as wintry wind,—
Some dim remembrance of a ghostly dread
Which lingers still when faith itself is dead.

And, above all, through thund'rous wintry roar,
    And summer ripple, this, and this alone,
    For ever do I make this barren moan :—
No end, there is no end,—on Time's dull shore
I wail, I beat, I thunder, evermore.

———o———

BERLIN, 1871.

THE spring day was all of a flutter with flags ;
    The mad chimes were beating like surf in the air ;
The beggars had slunk out of sight with their rags ;
    And the balconies teemed with the rich and the fair.

And below, on each side, the long vistas were set
　In a frame-work of faces, patient and white,—
Wives, mothers, sweethearts, with full eyes wet,
　And sick hearts longing to see the sight.

Till at length, when the evening was waning, there ran
　A stir through the crowd, and far-off, like a flame,
The setting sun burned on the helms of the van,
　And with trampling of hoofs the proud conquerors
　　came.

And with every step they advanced, you might hear
　Women's voices, half maddened with long-deferred joy:
" Thank God ! he is safe.　See, my love, we are here !
　See ! here am I, darling; and this is our boy !"

Or, " Here am I, dearest, still faithful and true;
　Your own love as of old !"　Or an agonised cry,
As the loved face came not with the comrades she knew,
　And the rough soldiers found not a word to reply.

And pitiful hands led her softly away,
　With a loving heart rent and broken in twain;
And the triumph sweeps onward, in gallant array,—
　The life and the hope, the despair and the pain.

Where was it ?   In Egypt, Assyria, Greece, Rome ?
   Ages since, or to-day ; in the old world, or new ?
Who shall tell ?   From all time these strange histories
   come ;
   And to-day, as of old, the same story is true.

And the long line sweeps past, and the dull world
   rolls on
Though the rapture is dead and the sad tears are dry ;
And careless of all, till the progress be done,
   Life rides like a conqueror triumphing by.

———o———

THE BEACON.

FAIR shines the beacon from its lonely rock,
   Stable alone amid the unstable waves :
In vain the surge leaps with continual shock,
   In vain around the wintry tempest raves,
   And ocean thunders in her sounding caves.

For here is life within the gate of death,
  Calm light and warmth amid the storm without;
Here sleeping love breathes with untroubled breath,
  And faith, clear-eyed, pierces the clouds of doubt
  And monstrous depths which compass her about.

So calm, so pure, yet prisoned and confined;
  Fenced by white walls from pleasure as from pain.
Not always glooms the sea or shrieks the wind :
  Sometimes light zephyrs curl the azure main,
  And the sweet sea-nymphs glide with all their train.

Or Aphrodite rises from the foam,
  And lies all rosy on the golden sand,
And o'er the purple plains the Nereids roam;
  Sweet laughter comes borne from the joyous band,
  And faint sweet odours from the far-off land.

And straightway the impatient soul within
  Loathes its white house which to a jail doth turn;
Careless of true or false, of right or sin,
  Careless of praying hands or eyes that burn,
  Or aught that sense can feel or mind discern.

Knowing but this,—that the unknown is blest,
  Holding delight of free untrammelled air :
Delight of toil sweeter than any rest,
    Fierce storms with cores of calm for those who dare,
    Black rayless nights than fairest noons more fair.

And drifting forth at eve in some frail boat,
  Beholds the old light, like a setting star,
Sink in the sea, and still doth fare and float
    Adown the night till day-break shows afar,—
    And hark the faint low thunders of the bar.

Nor if indeed he reach the land of rest,
  Nor if those pitiless crests shall plunge him down,
Knows he ; but whether breathless azure smile,
    Or furious night and horrible tempests frown,
    Living or dying, Freedom wears a crown.

——o——

THE GARDEN OF REGRET.

BEYOND the dim walls of the shadowy past,
  A sweet vague host of fancies flourishes,
Like garden seeds in some rough hollow cast,
  Which all unasked the kind earth nourishes,
And sends up tender blooms more sweet and fair
Than the dull present rears with all its care.

There on its thin stem hangs the frail white flower ;
  Far sweeter now she shines within the shade,
Than when of old within the trim kept bower
  And perfumed lush parterres her home she made ;
Because her sister blooms are past and gone,
And this alone it is that lingers on.

The same white flower,—but oh, the depths of change !
  Before, the creamy petals, broad and strong,
Were all adust with gold, and filled with strange
  Sweet scents, which lurked the odorous depths among :
Deep in her honeyed wells, the bee would stay
Content, and birds sing round the live-long day.

The same white flower—yet changed in scent and hue.
  Now the fair feeble petals curl and shrink ;
The dead smooth surfaces are veined with blue ;
  No honeyed draughts they hold for bee to drink,
Nor busy hum, nor joyous song is heard.
What hath she left to charm or bee or bird ?

Only a faint sweet odour lingers yet,
  Dearer than those rich scents of former years ;
A fragile fairness, fairer through regret,
  And watered by the dewy fount of tears.
To me that outcast flower is dearer grown,
Than when in those fair gardens overblown.

I set her in the garden of my heart,
  And water her from life's sincerest spring ;
And lo ! once more the frail stems quicken and start,
  Fair honeyed blooms arise and blithe birds sing :
The old sweet flower in scent and gorgeous hue,
But not the tender grace that once I knew.

Alas ! not in the present will she grow :
  The present has its own blooms sweet and bright ;

Within its four walls life's fair pleasures blow,
　And each gay season brings its own delight :
Far off in dewy shades the exile sweet
Grows fair, and paths untrodden by living feet.

There let her stay.　I know not if my theme
　Be love, or some fair child of heart or mind :
Young friendships, hopes, beliefs, which like a dream
　Pass from us leaving some sweet ghost behind.
Leave them behind, they have been ; others are.
And shall be.　Lo ! the spring time is not far.

NEW NOVELS

PUBLISHED BY

HENRY S. KING & CO.

I.
CRUEL AS THE GRAVE.
By the COUNTESS VON BOTHMER.   Three vols.,
crown 8vo.   [*Just out.*

II.
HER TITLE OF HONOUR.
(Second Edition.) By HOLME LEE. Author of
" Kathie Brande," "For Richer for Poorer," etc.
One vol., crown 8vo.

III.
HALF A DOZEN DAUGHTERS.
By J. MASTERMAN.   Author of "A Fatal Error."
Two vols., crown 8vo.

IV.
WHOSE WIFE IS SHE?
By SYDNEY MOSTYN.   Crown 8vo.   [*Immediately.*

V.
MANQUÉE.
By ALICE FISHER, Author of "Too Bright to Last."
                                    [*Shortly.*

VI.
THOMASINA.
By the author of "Dorothy," "De Cressy," etc.
                                    [*Shortly.*

VII.
LINKED AT LAST.
By F. E. BUNNETT.   Translator of Berthold Auer-
bach's "On the Heights," etc.   One vol., crown 8vo.
                                  [*In a few days.*

VIII.
A GOOD MATCH.
By AMELIA PERRIER.   Author of "Mea Culpa."
                                  [*Immediately.*

65, Cornhill, London.

Henry S. King & Co.'s New Books.

I.

THE SECRET OF LONG LIFE. Dedicated by special permission to LORD ST. LEONARDS. Handsomely bound in bevelled boards, large crown 8vo, 5s.

II.

EASTERN EXPERIENCES. By L. BOWRING, C.S.I., Lord Canning's Private Secretary, and for many years the principal Commissioner of Mysore and Coorg. In one vol., handsome demy 8vo, illustrated with Maps and Diagrams. 16s.

III.

WESTERN INDIA BEFORE AND DURING THE MUTINIES. Pictures drawn from Life. By Major-General Sir GEORGE LE GRAND JACOB, K.C.S.I., C.B., Late Special Political Commissioner, Southern Mahratta Country, etc., etc., in one vol., crown 8vo, 7s. 6d.

IV.

THE DIVINE KINGDOM ON EARTH AS IT IS IN HEAVEN. In demy 8vo, cloth, 10s. 6d. "Our COMMONWEALTH is in Heaven."

V.

JOURNALS KEPT IN FRANCE AND ITALY, from 1848 to 1852. With a Sketch of the Revolution of 1848. By the late NASSAU WILLIAM SENIOR. Edited by his daughter, M. C. M. SIMPSON. In two vols., post 8vo, 24s.

VI.

THE NILE WITHOUT A DRAGOMAN. (Second Edition.) By FREDERIC EDEN. In one vol., crown 8vo, cloth, 7s. 6d.

VII.

DISCIPLINE AND DRILL. Four Lectures delivered to the London Scottish Rifle Volunteers. By Captain S. FLOOD PAGE, Adjutant of the Regiment, late 105th Light Infantry, and Adjutant of the Edinburgh Rifle Brigade. Fcap. 8vo, cloth gilt, 2s. 6d.

65, Cornhill, London.

VIII.

ASPROMONTE, AND OTHER POEMS. (Second Edition.) Cloth, 4s. 6d.

IX.

THE INN OF STRANGE MEETINGS, AND OTHER POEMS. By MORTIMER COLLINS. Crown 8vo, 5s.

X.

THE EUROPEAN IN INDIA. A Hand-book of practical information for those proceeding to, or residing in, the East Indies, relating to Outfits, Routes, Time for Departure, Indian Climate, etc. By EDMUND C. P. HULL. To which is added—A MEDICAL GUIDE FOR ANGLO-INDIANS. Being a compendium of Advice to Europeans in India, relating to the Preservation and Regulation of Health. By R. S. MAIR, M.D., F.R.C.S.E., late Deputy Coroner of Madras. In one vol., post 8vo, 6s.

XI.

SCRIPTURE LANDS IN CONNECTION WITH THEIR HISTORY. By G. S. DREW, M.A., Rector of Avington, Winchester, Author of "Reasons of Faith," "Scripture Studies," etc. Second Edition, bevelled boards, 8vo, price 10s. 6d.

WORKS BY THE REV. STOPFORD A. BROOKE, M.A.

I.

FREEDOM IN THE CHURCH OF ENGLAND. (Second Edition.) Six Sermons suggested by the Voysey Judgment. In One Volume. Crown 8vo, cloth, 3s. 6d.

II.

SERMONS PREACHED IN ST. JAMES'S CHAPEL, YORK STREET. Post 8vo, 6s. Fifth Edition.

III.

A NEW VOLUME OF SERMONS is in the Press, and will shortly appear.

Books Preparing for Publication.

I.
ECHOES OF A FAMOUS YEAR.
A New Work by HARRIET PARR. Author of " The Life of Jeanne d'Arc," etc.

II.
THE PASTOR OF THE DESERT.
A Book for the Young. From the French of Eugène Pelletan. Translated by Colonel E. P. DE L'HOSTE. Handsomely bound, in crown 8vo, with an engraved frontispiece, price 5s.

III.
THE DREAM AND THE DEED, AND OTHER POEMS.
By PATRICK SCOTT. Author of " Footpaths between two Worlds." Crown 8vo, 4s. 6d.

IV.
ROUND THE WORLD IN 1870.
A Volume of Travels. By A. D. CARLISLE. Illustrated with Maps. Demy 8vo, 16s.

V.
THE WAY TO WIN.
A Book for the Young.

VI.
STREAMS FROM HIDDEN SOURCES.

VII.
MEMOIRS of the COUNTESS LEONORA CHRISTINA,
Of Schleswig Holstein—Countess Ulfeldt. Translated from the German by F. E. BUNNÈTT, translator of Grimm's " Life of Michael Angelo," etc.

HENRY S. KING & CO., 65, CORNHILL, LONDON.

www.ingramcontent.com/pod-product-compliance
Lightning Source LLC
Chambersburg PA
CBHW030407270326
41926CB00009B/1305